The Poor Poet

*Poetry that engages the soul, the mind,
and the funny bone.*

D0896321

Rich Reardon

ISBN: 978-0-578-82154-2

TABLE OF CONTENTS

DEDICATION

Karen Scott and I were married on August 22, 1970. I thought it was the best day of my life, but it continued getting better for thirty-two years until she passed away January 8, 2003. We not only adored each other, but were the best of buddies. As voracious readers and researchers, our bookshelves reflect a love of history, art, literature, and gourmet cooking.

At a private school in Tampa, Karen taught every phase of history beginning with ancient medieval. Her students reaped the benefits of her passion for making distinct connections between history, culture, and the arts. Her colleagues described her as a whirlwind at school, rarely sitting still. She was like that at home, too—continually moving from one project to the next.

We collected over 950 cookbooks and enjoyed studying a broad variety of cuisines. We started with Mexican and moved to French. Then while taking a class on Italian language and culture, we delved into Italian dishes. Next, we researched and prepared Greek, Mediterranean, Chinese, Thai, and Indian foods. We created many of our own recipes. I smile when I remember the two of us bustling around our kitchen, smelling the rich aromas, and then dining by candlelight. Just the two of us.

This book is dedicated to Karen and the beautiful memories of our life together.

1

FOR KAREN

WHIMSEYS

In the early 90's I got in the habit of writing daily poems for Karen. I referred to myself as the Morning Poet. This was not great poetry. I often had a difficult time coming up with a topic. I would use something her students were studying in her history classes, or something that had happened to us or someone we knew, or what was in the news that day. Sometimes the poem was about not being able to come up with a topic. It didn't matter. What was important was the effort to create a special gift for her—a poem that only the two of us would understand.

Karen saved each scrap of paper the poems were written on. I found the entire collection after she was gone, and I hesitated looking at them because I thought it would be too painful. But when I finally began reading these simple poems, I was able to smile and remember special moments of our life together. I've included some that were just about us but mostly her.

We celebrated our anniversary every month.

THE POOR POET

The finest gift I ever got,
When your daddy made you mine,
It is a gift that keeps on giving,
Happy Three Hundred Twenty-Nine.

I sit here every morning,
Writing poems upon demand,
A blank page there before me,
With pen clenched tight in hand,
My brain is fairly reeling,
Deep thoughts run through my head,
But when the pen and paper meet,
Pure tripe comes out instead.
Today we both can celebrate,
Number Three Hundred Forty-Four,
But I'm not satisfied with that,
I want a thousand more.

Before I put that ring on you,
I was really never alive,
So now, I say my age in months,
Is Three Hundred Sixty-Five.

Her first glorious smile of the day was always special to me.

Morning's a time for beautiful things,
It begins with the sun's first ray,
And the loveliest thing I ever saw,
Is her first smile of the day.

Oh what's my reward in this life,
What makes it all worthwhile?
The answer, Dear, is obvious,
It's Karen's morning smile.

There are some things I cannot see,
But still, I know are there,
'Cause every time I look at you,
There's magic in the air.

"Another day in Paradise,"
That has a lovely sound,
But every place is Paradise,
As long as you're around.

Valentines will soon be here,
And so I'd better start,
It takes more days than one to show,
What's really in my heart.

Life has been a breeze for me,
I've always had an anchor,
One life isn't time enough,
For me to ever thank her.

Miracles are everywhere,
I know that this is true,
I have a big one in my life,
That miracle is You.

THE POOR POET

Since the day I got,
To lift your veil,
You've been the breeze,
That fills my sail.

A birthday's a time to celebrate,
Our many gifts, it's true,
So the twenty-third of April,
Is more for me than you.

Karen's birthday was April 23.

My life is full of happiness,
Living here with you,
I don't know how to love you more,
But every day, I do.

TO KAREN

The winter wind can blow the snow, but I don't feel the cold,
I'm full of love for one young girl, she'll warm me 'til we're
    old,
The stings of life are blunted now, the skies are blue not grey,
The dark of night, the unknown fright, they all have gone
    their way.

It's strange somehow that though my eyes are blinded to all
    pain,
They now perceive the joys of life as cleansed by summer
    rain,

The cloudy days are brighter now, the birds compose new
    songs,
I'm now inspired to try my best to right uncounted wrongs.

Our love has changed the world for me, I see new things
    each day,
I notice flowers, feel new joys in watching children play,
The moon just seems to glow for us, the stars now brighter
    shine,
I find new thrills in simple things, and happiness is mine.

How can one woman do these things, I'm sure I'll never
    know,
I'm only sure I'll pledge my life to pay this debt I owe,
She's just the perfect mate for me, she fits me like a glove,
She's tenderness, she's sweet caress, she's hope and she is love.

And when I've ended my days here, and shed this mortal
    skin,
In eulogy they'll say of me, "He knew the way to win,
He had good fortune all his days, he led a wond'rous life,
He was the happiest of men, for Karen was his wife.

THE POOR POET

I wrote the following poems for and about Karen after she died.

MY YELLOW ROSE

My Yellow Rose is gone from me,
A victim of the frost,
When winter's wind has scourged the land,
And everything seems lost,
The world is bleak and featureless,
And life is bare in scope,
My garden is in dormancy,
Without a ray of hope.

I don't believe in what they say,
That deep down in the earth,
Is a seed of love that holds within,
The promise of rebirth.

Late winter winds keep up the chill,
But the sun peeps through the clouds,
And occasionally, a burst of warmth,
Will thaw away the shrouds,
The garden's still in silence now,
But in the new sun's beams
Are rays of hope awakening,
From unremembered dreams.

Perhaps there's truth in what they say,
That deep down in the earth,
Is a seed of love that holds within,
The promise of rebirth.

Rich Reardon

The early spring brings verdant hues,
With buds and sprigs of grass,
The snow is all but melted now,
As the pain of loss will pass,
And though I never shall forget,
What my Rose meant to me,
I've come in time to realize,
That what will be will be.

I think there's truth in what they say,
That deep down in the earth,
Is a seed of love that holds within,
The promise of rebirth.

My garden's filled with beauty now,
The flowers bloom in May,
And though my Yellow Rose is gone,
She left me a bouquet,
I see her vision everywhere,
She's watching, I suppose,
The glory here reminds me of,
My Blue-Eyed Yellow Rose.

I know now what they say is true,
That deep down in the earth,
Is a seed of love that holds within,
The promise of rebirth.

Virtus junxit, mors non separabat.
(Virtue joins, death does not separate)

THE POOR POET

Karen and I had the most magical marriage I ever saw. It just got better every day. When she died on Jan. 8, 2003, I was, and still remain, crestfallen. I wanted to honor her in some way. I tried to cover the grief process from rage and denial through acceptance and possible hope. I also feel we humans live in cycles with the earth. In other words, Christmas could never be in the summer because the time for a new beginning is the winter solstice, and Easter could never be in the fall because the time for a rebirth is the spring. These symbols are ingrained into our psyche. Yellow roses were her favorite, so I used the rose as a metaphor.

TWO YEARS LATER

The hollow man plods down the road,
Just taking things in stride,
With emptiness surrounding him,
And emptiness inside.

For many years his life was bliss,
No heeding of the cost,
The greater gifts we get in life,
The greater pain when lost.

She made him better than he was,
T'was summer in the sun,
Together they were more than two,
Alone he's less than one.

The world was filled with happiness,
They thought that it would last,
They dreamed about the future,
Now he dreams about the past.

This one was a catharsis for me. Trying to express my feelings two years after Karen died.

AESTHETICS

Beauty fills this world of ours,
We find it all around,
It comes to us in sight and smell,
In taste and touch and sound.

The last red rose of summertime,
First crocus of the spring,
That magic loving moment when,
The finger gets the ring.

A verse by Keats or Coleridge,
Or a sonnet by the Bard,
The heartfelt grief and sympathy,
Of a sweet condolence card.

The hope and glee of Christmas time,
A pure cathedral bell,
A Madonna and her precious babe,
From the brush of Raphael.

THE POOR POET

The salty tang of caviar,
The bubbles of champagne,
The perfume of a fresh mown lawn,
Or a forest in the rain.

The laughter of a child at play,
The love song of a lark,
A happy clan reunion,
With a picnic in the park.

On a steamy summer evening,
The cool breeze of a fan,
The smell of morning coffee,
Or of bacon in the pan.

But of all the beauty I've known,
The one most pure and true,
The one that makes my life complete,
That perfect one is you.

ANSWERED PRAYERS

I wished to find the ideal mate,
To share my future, share my fate,
The one to love in every way,
And then I first saw you that day.

I had the perfect one in mind,
Ever gentle, ever kind,

The one to always see it through,
I turned around and there was you.

I hoped that I could find the best,
One who'd live a life with zest,
One for whom I'd always care,
The door was opened, you were there.

I dreamed that I could find the One,
A life of laughter, joy, and fun,
True and loving all the while,
I spoke the words and saw you smile.

EARLY MORNING

Early in the morning time, before the sun comes up,
I get the coffee perking and I have my morning cup.

I'll let my bride sleep in a while, before she has to go,
My life revolves around that girl because I love her so.

And then I creep into our room, a swelling in my heart,
I bring along her coffee cup, to give her day a start.

I softly nuzzle on her cheek and whisper in her ear,
Remind her of our memories that both of us hold dear.

I gently lead her to the world, her consciousness restored,
And that is when my day begins, I get my great reward.

With eyes still closed and half asleep, she gives that crooked
  grin,
I feel a charge deep in my soul, a power surge within.

I now will have the strength to face the trials along the way,
It's that first smile, that lovely smile, the best one of the day.

*I always thought that first smile was the loveliest of all of them,
perhaps because I was the only one who ever saw it. It was MINE
and mine alone.*

HOME

My home is like a fortress strong,
A castle, wise men say,
Protection from the outside world,
From evils of the day.

At home I am surrounded by,
The warmth of tender care,
Filled with laughter and with love,
And memories we share.

When I am gone away from here,
No matter where I roam,
No matter what I'm doing there,
My thoughts are all of home.

But now I'm in a different world,
This place has lost its thrill,
When I am home and you are gone,
Then I am homesick still.

So now it finally comes to me,
That whether near or far,
My home is not a place at all,
It's anywhere you are.

SHE WAS
A Sonnet

She was the reason I was born,
She was the anchor to my keel,
She was my rose without a thorn,
She was my guide, my pilot's wheel.

She was my lovely peaceful dove,
She was the cloak that kept me warm,
She was my angel from above,
She was my shelter from the storm.

While she was here my life was bliss,
But now she's gone and I'm bereft,
My life is something that's amiss,
And emptiness is all that's left.

A sail-less ship on torpid seas,
I'm grateful for my memories.

THE FOUNTAIN

There's a fountain in the desert, and it flows but once a year,
It mostly sleeps there deep beneath the crust,
The land around bereft of life, stark, and brown, and gray,
Oppressive heat, and rock, and sand, and dust.

But then upon a certain day, a stream will trickle forth,
And suddenly the land begins to bloom,
Green sprigs will begin to rise and colors will emerge,
And beauty now replaces doom and gloom.

The contrast is of epic scope, a scene of life or death,
It seems as if the life has won the day,
But then as it does every year, the fountain water stops,
And all that beauty slowly fades away.

My world is like the desert there, the fountain like my love,
When she is gone, then all is dark with strife,
But when she graces, all is changed,
My world is filled with beauty, joy, and life.

THE OATH

Though she's been gone these many years,
Near half a score plus three,
Yet not one time have I forgot,
Just what she meant to me.

Friends have said that I should find,
Another one to share,
But that would be impossible,
For no one could compare.

She was too perfect in my mind,
In every way I know,
She rests upon that pedestal,
I worship from below.

I spend my days within the past,
I thrive on memories,
Content to wait in solitude,
With my sweet reveries.

I'll never find a love like hers,
So pure, so sweet, so fine,
When I swore "Til us death do part,"
The death I meant was mine.

VISIONS

He sees her vision everywhere,
She's always on his mind,
She gave him everything in life,
He now repays in kind.

He hears her voice in every breeze,
So gentle, soft and sweet,
Reminding him of happy times,
That made his life complete.

Their interplay is magical,
Like when they were a team,
Her spirit has remained behind,
In every thought and dream.

He keeps his visions to himself,
So no one else will see,
Stoic in his interplay,
No need for company.

His heart is filled with joy and love,
He has a face of stone,
He spends his days in solitude,
But never is alone.

MOON DREAMS

I had that dream again last night,
The one when you are here,
It is my favorite dream of all,
I love it when you're near.

I saw your smile, and gentle eyes,
I felt your scented breath,
And in my dream the doctors erred,
And you had cheated death.

But when I wake, my dreaming ends,
It all comes back to me,
It's morning now and I must face,
The harsh reality.

But oh that dream, that lovely dream,
It felt so real and strong,
It lingered in my heart and mind,
I've smiled the whole day long.

I love the time I spend with you,
Beneath the silver moon,
I hope I have that dream again,
Tonight . . . or some night soon.

MONUMENT

I thought I loved you when we met,
But I was wrong.

I thought I loved you when we wed,
But I was wrong again.

In hindsight, through the lens of time,
I see those things as they have been,
And I have come to realize,
I did not know what love was then.

I now know love's a living thing,
That needs a constant nourishment,
It slowly builds upon itself,
An ever-growing monument.

Each day I think I've reached the peak,
The apogee of happiness,

But when the next day comes, I find,
That yesterday was something less.

Today I'm basking in the bliss,
I feel you plucking my heart strings,
Anticipating even more,
Finding what tomorrow brings.

THE OLD MAN

The man walks down the road alone,
Each movement is a strain,
The muscles are in disrepair,
Each step creates new pain.

He gently smiles at passersby,
With kindness from within,
One cannot see the lion there,
That once was in his skin.

In youth he knew the joys of life,
A treasure 'neath the sun,
Existence had a meaning then,
The day he met The One.

They had a love, a boundless love,
They pushed the limits far,
They touched the moon with happiness,
And then they touched each star.

Together they scaled mountains high,
And sailed the stormy seas,
But now he's merely grateful for,
His stardust memories.

An autobiography of sorts. Just getting by without my beloved wife.

2

BIRTHDAYS

SEXAGENARIAN

Sitting in the park and playing checkers with the boys,
Trees and bushes screening out the loud unwanted noise,
Watching all the girlies pass, tall and slim and sleek,
Makes me feel as old as hell, makes me feel a freak.

Once I was a dandy stud and held myself with pride,
Once I broke a lot of hearts and terrified my bride,
Once I was a rooster cock, the goal of every hen,
Once I was the knave of hearts, the ideal man of men.

Winning days are over now, cannot place or show,
Where I once stood tall and strong, today I'm hanging low,
Gone's the spark that drove me on, or I'd be scoring yet,
Guess I'll go back home and play with my erector set.

This was written for my Dad on his sixtieth birthday. We had a big family reunion for the event.

Rich Reardon

MY SWEET BABY SISTER

The sun it is setting, the wind it is cold,
My sweet baby sister is 30 years old,
This fact it is shocking, this fact gives me fears,
'Til now I'd forgotten I'm adding up in years,
I'm over the hill now and way past my prime,
At home with the Waltons is now a good time,
I've fallen into that old "elderly" trap,
That one of life's thrills is to take a good crap,
So take some advice from a man who is gray,
Have fun while you can Sis, and have a big day,
Rejoice in those age spots, enjoy every wrinkle,
I'd better quit now 'cause I have to go tinkle.

TO A LADY ON HER FORTIETH BIRTHDAY

The Princess moved through life just like a monorail through
    Disneyland,
As effortless and easy as can be,
It was living in the meadowland of chocolate milk and honey
    cakes,
Where the champagne and the caviar were free.

But then one day she came upon an obstacle to reckon with,
A river which was just a bit too wide,
And a grubby little feller with a ferry boat and sign that read,
"I'm the way to see the other side."

He was an ugly little codger in a grimy sleazy overcoat,
His mug was sorta wrinkly like a prune,
His teeth were just a mem'ry and his hands were shriveled up,
And his head was bald and bumpy like the moon.

Well the Princess dimpled sweetly at this little elder
    statesman,
And she asked him, "Howdy, what's the story Bro?"
He said, "The river's name is Apathy, the boat is Ancient Age,
And Honey Babe, my handle is Four-O.

As we boogie on through life Hon, we gotta pay the piper,
And today's the first collection, that's the truth,
The journey 'cross the water, it don't cost a single nickel,
Sweetie, all you gotta give me is your youth."

Well, the Princess got to thinking 'bout this crazy twist in life,
And she tried to figure out another plan,
She had a Masters in Finagle and a Doctorate in Guile,
So she reckoned she could fool the little man.

Then she said, "Let's have a party with a couple kegs of brew,
I would like another fling before I go,
We can order up some pizzas and some pretzels and some
    nuts,"
This all sounded pretty tasty to Four-O.

So they got the party going and the suds were flowing free,
And the geezer got besotted by the brew,
When the sun was straight above the Princess put her

scheme to work,
She said, "I think it's getting warmer here, don't you?

I would dearly love to cool off in that stream that's flowing by,
I'd dearly love to quench my body's thirst,
We'll romp around and splash around like little baby fishies,
We'll both go in, but Sugar, you go first."

So Four-O hit the water and he paddled all about,
'Til he finally reached the river's middle line,
And he hollered back at Princess, saying, "Man this hits the
    spot,
Come in Tootsie Pie, the water's fine."

Then the Princess took a running leap and landed on his
    head,
From there she leaped again and ne'er got wet,
She hit the bank a running and left Four-O in the drink,
For all I know, he's swimming 'round there yet.

The moral of this story is a simple one indeed,
This birthday stuff is strictly in the mind,
If you hit Four-O a running and you're watching where you
    step,
You'll leave Old Age and Apathy behind.

*For my beloved sister, Robin, on that fateful day. She must have
taken my advice because to this day, she has not reached forty years
of age in looks or deportment.*

THE LADY

The Lady Laughs

She sees great pleasure everywhere,
She always has a smile,
She spends each day with mirth and joy,
And laughing all the while.

The Lady Lives

She gives each day all that she has,
Ignoring stress and strife,
She sees the good in everyone,
She takes big bites of life.

The Lady Loves

I think that in her childhood she,
Was struck by cupid's dart,
Of all the folks I've ever known,
She has the purest heart.

The Lady Gives

The most unselfish soul on earth,
She holds me in her thrall,
She gave to me her daughter's hand,
The greatest gift of all.

To Karen's mother, my Second Mom. This truly describes that amazing lady.

Rich Reardon

HAPPY BIRTHDAY, SCOTTY

When a fellow reaches fifty,
It's like falling off a cliff,
His middle joint grows limber,
His other joints grow stiff.

He goes to bed quite early now,
And spends time in the can,
Each morning there's a dish of prunes,
Thank God for Raisin Bran.

His mind starts playing tricks on him,
His hair starts falling out,
His eyes will turn to bleariness,
Can't hear you, 'less you shout.

Younger folks will laugh at him.
As a senile, mindless jerk,
His body will betray him and,
What doesn't hurt won't work.

But there's a hope for Scotty now,
It's there for all to see,
Something to look forward to,
A colonoscopy.

For my nephew, Scotty, when he finally became eligible for AARP.

3

WEDDINGS

WEDDING SONG

We're holding hands together,
On this, our wedding day,
Friends and family here with us,
To help us on our way.

Chorus:

We're standing here before them,
We both have made our choice,
And now we have a lifetime,
A lifetime to rejoice.

Today is our beginning,
It's when the true love starts,
This is a holy sacrament,
The joining of two hearts.

Chorus

If children come to bless us,
We'll share them with each other,
The best gift I can give them,
Is deeply love their mother.

Chorus

As we start our life together,
And face the rising sun,
I promise you in front of all,
The courting's just begun.

Chorus

Like a Christmas carol, I always wanted to write a wedding song. This is my idea of how a marriage works best – never quit courting. The greatest gift we get in this life is that one person with whom to travel the road.

THE BEST OF DAYS
A Sonnet

Orange blossoms, sweet perfume,
Perfect beauty, pure white dress,
Friends and family fill the room,
Smiling pastor, here to bless

Careful planning, years of dreams,
Joyful families, posted banns,
Stained glass colors warm sun's beams,
Eager couple, joining hands.

Two new titles, husband, wife,
Vows are made, they understand,
Start a family, loving life,
Live in bliss, as Heaven planned.

The day she glided down the aisle,
The day their world became worth-while.

BRETT AND BRENDA

The greatest gift we ever get,
In this life 'neath the sun,
Is when two souls decide to merge,
When two turns into one.

A life of joy ahead of them,
And loving all the while,
A reason for them both to greet,
Each morning with a smile.

So Brenda, Brett, two special hearts,
Each found the perfect mate,
Let's raise our glasses high above,
It's time to celebrate.

Dear friends, Brett and Brenda, were married on August 4, 2018. I recited this at their reception.

CONGRATULATIONS, JODI AND SCOTTY

A Cubs fan makes the perfect wife,
She always will be true,
Courage, strength, and fortitude,
For all that she's been through.

For longer than a century,
The team had won no flag,
Normal folks would be depressed,
And let their spirits sag.

But Cubby fans are valorous,
Demand another deal,
Pressure makes a diamond stone,
Heat produces steel.

Then finally, two years ago,
The drought came to a stop,
The years of grief were done at last,
The Cubs came out on top.

The glee and bliss were unconfined,
With dancing in the street,
A long and bitter winter makes,
The summer seem more sweet.

THE POOR POET

Today we're here to celebrate,
The joining of two hearts,
Scotty, Jodi, a life of love,
It's when the magic starts.

The Reardon clan is filled with joy,
And wish to give our thanks,
Welcome Jodi, and just for you,
God Bless Ernie Banks.

My nephew, Scotty was lucky enough to marry his love, Jodi, on March 24, 2018. Their reception took place at a Chicago Cubs spring practice game.

4

ANNIVERSARIES

A LOVE POEM—FORTY YEARS LONG

For forty long years you have shared bed and board,
You've lived with life's cheers and life's groans,
At times you have felt you were top of the world,
At times, just an old bag of bones.

It wasn't all easy, with three kids to raise,
At times it was all down the tubes,
To add to your problems, you had to admit,
That the three you were raising were boobs.

Your children were spared all your anguish and grief,
You led them with never a shove,
You showed them the way how to greet every day,
With humor, compassion, and love.

You never will know what an impact you made,
You've given three people a light,
That life can be based upon goodness and love,
And truth will illuminate night.

So forty long years, why it's not even half,
Of all the long years that we'd like,
This wish is for more with our love and our prayers,
From Robin, from Rich, and from Mike.

For my parents, Darrell and Helen, March 2, 1981. Their three kids collaborated on this: I wrote the poem, Robin calligraphed it, and Mike framed it.

TWO HEARTS

They were children of the Depression,
They knew both want and need,
They were part of that Great Generation,
Whose word was as good as their deed,
      Two hearts as one since Forty-One
      With a legacy of Hope.

They embarked on a life with each other,
As war clouds started to loom,
But through struggles and triumphs and setbacks,
They're still on their first honeymoon,
    Two harts as one since Forty-One,
    With a legacy of Joy.

When children came they labored,
To teach them right from wrong,
How to stand behind your principles,
How to keep your spirit strong,
    Two hearts as one since Forty-One,
    With a legacy of Spirit.

Rich Reardon

They taught of ethics and morals,
And to keep kind thoughts in your head,
But they never preached when they would teach,
They'd show us how instead,
Two hearts as one since Forty-One,
With a legacy of Light.

They taught to take big bites of life,
And to never do things by half,
That the finest cure for all of life's ills,
Is to let out a big belly laugh.
Two hearts as one since Forty-One,
With a legacy of laughter.

So friends, as we stand here together,
With glasses raised high above,
We salute their greatest lesson of all,
They showed us each how to love,
Two hearts as one since Forty-One,
With a legacy of love.

Two hearts as one since Forty-One,
And the legacy Lives on.

For my parents' sixtieth wedding anniversary celebration.

SAPHIRE ANNIVERSARY

For forty-five years,
They've fit like a glove,
A life of adventure,
And laughter and love.

Their time has been happy,
They've lived out their dream,
Because they're together,
And worked as a team.

At times separated,
But never apart,
Ee're true to each other,
And true to each heart.

To have such dear friends,
To share all their bliss,
It just can't improve,
Or get better than this

GOLDEN DAY

Gold – the valued element,
The symbol of the best.
The medal of all winners and,
Of those who beat the test.

Rich Reardon

The cornerstone of human wealth,
The sign of quality,
But most of all, most precious gold,
The anniversary.

The greatest of accomplishments,
You've made the most of time,
Commitment is your way of life,
Results have been sublime.

You solved the question of great bliss,
It's simple in the end,
You showed the way to everyone,
You married your best friend.

For Bill and Robin, with pride, love, and deep respect

6-6-1970 to 6-6-2020
L = Au (50 equals gold)

5

HOLIDAYS

THE GIFT

It happened many years ago,
In a distant foreign land,
There was a birth in poverty,
That made men understand.

A baby in a manger lay,
The child was stable born,
And through his birth the dismal night,
Became the perfect morn.

Shepherds came to honor him
While angels came to sing,
The glory of all heaven chimed,
To herald the new king.

Three men came from eastern lands,
By following a star,
Gifts they brought, but the baby child,
Was a better gift by far.

The gift he brought that fateful night,
Was epic in its scope,
The gift he gave to all mankind:
The majesty of hope.

A CHRISTMAS TOAST

We're gathered here to celebrate the most amazing birth,
Of the Son of Man, who came down here to save our souls
    on earth,
And the proof that he existed, to save our world from gloom,
Can be found in all the love and joy that's right here in this
    room.

This one made my mother cry so I'm proud of it.

CHRISTMAS WISH

May these holidays bring you the things you desire,
May you have a big yule log to stuff in your fire,
May eight tiny reindeer camp out on your roof,
May your holiday spirits be ninety-six proof.

May Santa leave most of his sack at your tree,
May you have happy days full of good company,
May the rest of the year be a holiday treat,
May your stocking be crammed full of goodies, not feet.

On the eve of the New Year, when you plan to roam,
May your wife remain sober, so she can drive home,

May you have all your wishes and win all your bets,
And on New Year's Day, may you have no regrets.

WHAT CHRISTMAS CARDS SHOULD SAY

It must be Christmas time again,
'Cause all the billboards shout it,
Perhaps your dreams will all come true,
Maybe.....but I doubt it.

With Santa Claus on every corner,
Christmas must be close at hand,
It means Salvation Army carols,
Lovely cause, but lousy band.

Too much turkey, too much booze,
Have a dozen pounds to lose,
Have a million bills to pay,
Merry Christmas, anyway.

TWO LIGHTS

The earth was covered in dark despair,
The world was shrouded in sin,
Then the Lord in Heaven looked down and said,
"Behold, the new world begins,"

Chorus:
Two lights shone bright on that ancient night,

Rich Reardon

In that humble holy place,
One was a beacon to guide the way,
The other, a sweet glow of grace.

The beacon hung high in the evening sky,
To lead three men from afar,
From lands in the east they came bearing gifts,
As they followed that wonderous star.

Chorus

The glow of grace from a manger came,
To herald the birth of a king,
The magi and shepherds all gathered below,
To hear Heaven's angels sing.

Chorus

The world was changed on that fateful night,
No longer the fire and the sword,
The sins of the ages were washed away,
By the blood of the lamb of the Lord.

Chorus

Two lights still shine after all these years,
Together and never apart,
They can be seen every Christmas Day,
If you look deep down in your heart.

Chorus

I love the idea of Christmas and the wonderful music it brings.

I wanted to write a Christmas carol, but never cared for the modern songs with a rock theme. I have an idea of a tune for this, but I can't read or write music.

HORRORS

The night, a dark and dreary one,
When I was home alone,
I saw some sights, I heard some sounds,
That chilled me to the bone.

A group of ghosts were haunting me,
And then a ghoul was there,
A gorgon stood in front of me,
With snakes in place of hair.

A vampire came and wanted blood,
I heard a banshee's wail,
A werewolf wished to tear my flesh,
I thought my heart would fail.

A harpy shot her deadly bolt,
And then there was a troll,
A zombie of the living dead,
Prepared to take my soul.

I thought my life was over then,
My mind must be deranged,
But then, there were new visitors,
And everything was changed.

An angel and a fairy princess,
Trick or treating at my door,
All those monsters now forgotten,
I'll be frightened, Nevermore.

THANKSGIVING

We came from foreign climes across,
Those dark and stormy seas,
We sought a land where we could live,
And worship as we please.

We found this place, we set our roots,
And then began our toil,
Through diligence, the earth gave up,
The bounty of the soil.

We had a meal of gratitude,
To thank the Lord above,
To recognize the way that He,
Abides us with his love.

Today we gather for the feast,
Of turkey and of dressing,
The Great Provider gets our thanks,
For every single blessing.

Thanksgiving is a prayer of grace,
For the land of liberty,
America, America,
God shed His grace on thee.

NEW YEAR'S DAY

It's resolution time again,
A time to start anew,
My vices, they are numerous,
My virtues, they are few.

But I will change the way things are,
And become a better man,
I have a firmness deep inside,
And now I'm, sure I can.

I'll cast off all those sins of old,
I've found a certain cure,
My resolutions are resolved,
And I'll be Simon pure.

But I have said this many times,
Each New Year in the past,
And all my good intentions fail,
They never seem to last.

If history is any guide,
When this new year is done,
I will have made the same mistakes,
Because they're so much fun.

Rich Reardon

GO TELL IT ON THE MOUNTAIN
(Easter Version)

Chorus:
Go tell it on the mountain,
Over the hills and everywhere,
Go tell it on the mountain,
That Jesus Christ is Lord.

He bore the cross of sorrow,
Along the street of tears,
On Calvary He perished,
To end all people's fears.

Chorus

They came to do Him honor,
That third and fateful day,
The humble cave was empty,
The stone was moved away.

Chorus

He has returned in glory,
To show eternal love,
He has returned to lead us,
To God's grace up above.

Chorus

6

FAREWELL

MY DREAM

Last night I heard God chuckle,
It was in a dream I had,
Our Father up in Heaven,
Was laughing with my Dad.

The two of them were joshing,
With dear and long lost friends,
And then and there I realized,
True friendship never ends.

They were having such a jolly time,
Swapping tall old tales,
But as I stood apart, I felt,
The wind go from my sails.

There they were together,
And there I was alone,
I longed to gather up the gang,
And bring them all back home.

Then the Lord looked down upon me,
And He spoke into my heart,
He said, "Your Dad has never left,
No need to feel apart.

He's with you every day of life,
He's there each breath you take,
He's a major force behind,
Decisions that you make.

He's watching everything you do,
From his place up above,
He's watching all his loved ones,
And he's sharing in their love.

I know you miss your Dear Old Dad,
But you must know My son,
The world's a sadder place these days,
But Heaven's much more fun."

Last night I heard God chuckle,
Best dream I ever had,
I love to see how close they were,
Our Father and my Dad.

My dad passed away on Dec. 27, 2001. He was a wonderful man with great humor and love. It was on his following birthday on March 9, 2002, that I woke up in the middle of the night with this one running through my head. It was for our family but I am proud that it has been used in over 15 funerals since then.

MARCH 9, 2017

One hundred times around the sun,
Has gone our spinning earth,
A century has come and gone,
Since our dear father's birth.

His life was filled with happiness,
With humor and aplomb,
The greatest gift he gave to us,
His deep love for our mom.

He never told, he always showed,
The way to live a life,
His honor and devotion to,
His children and his wife.

He's gone now, but his family,
Still dreams of days back when,
Our father will be sorely missed,
Until we meet again.

My dad would have been 100 years old on this day. This was for our family in his honor.

A NEW ANGEL

It rained the day my mother died,
With all her children gathered 'round,
It seemed that all of heaven cried,

With teardrops puddled on the ground,
But later on the sun came through,
And beamed upon our reveries,
Thus, all our lives began anew,
So grateful for our memories,
It was no time for grief or shrouds,
The angels love a gentle soul,
I know she's up above the clouds,
Throughout her life she paid the toll,
   I see her standing by the Gates,
   And smiling down, as one who waits.

My beloved mother passed away exactly one week after her 89th birthday. All of her children were gathered around to send her off. Less than a minute after she left us there was an immense thunder crack and the heavens opened. Later, the clouds passed away to a beautiful day. What wonderful memories.

ABSENT FRIENDS

Looking back at my school days,
I remember my best friend,
We shared adventures and setbacks,
We were both true to the end.

When school was done, we went our ways,
We left the past behind,
The years went by, then decades passed,
Our friendship slipped my mind.

I guess we each were occupied,
With family and wife,
Careers and scouts and little league,
We got sidetracked by life.

Then yesterday I met another,
Friend from those school days,
We talked about what's happened since,
We went our separate ways.

I asked about my old best friend,
I wished the latest word,
He said, "He passed on years ago,
I'm sorry, thought you'd heard."

Like me, I knew his family felt,
The shock and disbelief,
They gathered in their sadness then,
They shared their common grief.

Oh, he's been gone these many years,
I don't know when or how,
Their mourning faded long ago,
My grief is starting now.

One of the great sorrows of my high school reunion was finding for the first time that so many of my classmates were no longer with us. Many I hadn't thought of for years, but I was grieved by their passing. It was strange that even though their loved ones had come to grips with it while I was just beginning my grief.

Rich Reardon

GOODBYE MY FRIEND

Last night I dreamed of days gone by,
　　And things that might have been,
Of a friend of mine I cannot see,
　　And I'll not see again,
I wept with grief, with loss and rage,
　　With anger and with fear,
Just why was my friend gone from me,
　　And why am I still here?
But then I saw a man appear,
　　In robes of flowing white,
His eyes were old as firmament,
　　And they shimmered in the night,
He spoke and birds sang softly sweet,
　　He spoke and kittens purred,
He spoke and mothers lullabyed,
　　The gentlest ever heard.

"I've seen your tears of anger son,
　　I've felt your grief and pain,
I've heard your puzzled questions son,
　　I've come here to explain.
Where I come from, it's lovely there,
　　The air is filled with song,
But every now and then we feel,
　　That we've been dead too long,
And though each soul is beautiful,
　　And each has much to give,
Sometimes we need new blood, my son,

To teach us how to live,
We searched your world for such a soul,
    Who laughed away each strife,
Who faced each day with humor, son,
    Who loved each day of life,
Look in my eyes and you will see,
    That all I say is true,
You miss your friend, but oh my son,
    We need him more than you."

The sun rose up this morning,
    And the earth began anew,
The sky was clear without a cloud,
    The grass was fresh with dew,
With head held high I spoke into,
    The clear and crystal air,
"Goodbye my friend…goodbye,
    And teach them how to live up there."

*I lost a dear friend suddenly and unexpectedly to a heart attack.
This one was for his grieving family.*

LIFE STREAM – FOR CAROL

The smiling brook began her life,
High in a mountain spring,
Then bubbled down to lower climes,
And caused the birds to sing.

She made her journey over stones,
Meandering in her play,
She brought new life where'ere she went,
While laughing all the way.

She merged one day with another stream,
Which broadened out her shore,
Together they had richer lives,
And were stronger than before.

They nurtured all the land around,
All full of love and free,
And then upon a fateful day,
She reached the gentle sea.

She blended with the briny deep,
As part of the tide and foam,
All Heaven is rejoicing now,
An angel has come home.

Carol Merrill, a friend of my sister and brother-in-law, was a wonderful lady filled with laughter, love and a lust for life. She became a dear friend to me as well. We thought she had beaten her cancer after several years of struggle, but she passed away suddenly. I used the stream as a metaphor for a wonderful life. My sister read it at Carol's Celebration of Life.

LUCY

I have strong childhood memories,
Although it's really been a while,
And one stands out above the rest,
The neighbor lady with the beautiful smile,

She and her family had such warmth,
They always seemed so kind and wise,
I loved her then, I love her now,
The neighbor lady with the beautiful eyes.

Times will come and times will go,
For many years we've been apart,
But she is with me still today,
The neighbor lady with the beautiful heart.

Dedicated with love to Lucy Espinosa. She and Jim and Mary and Jimmy were the best neighbors we ever had and the finest family I've ever known.

MAXINE

I've known her over sixty years,
The love was at first sight,
Through all that time she's still the same,
Her star is shining bright.

She always had a smile for me,
She had a massive heart,
Her wealth was in experience,
With wisdom to impart.

Humor was her way of life,
I loved to see her smile,
A constant twinkle in her eye,
And laughing all the while.

I know she's looking down on us,
From Heaven up above,
She'll carry on her legacy,
Of sweet abiding love.

In honor of Maxine Newell, a true giant in my life.

MY SISTER'S FRIEND

I lost a good friend yesterday,
It's hard to understand,
Everything I knew of her,
I got it second-hand.

She was my sister's bosom friend,
Two kindred spirits true,
I heard her mentioned many times,
The Friend I Never Knew.

I heard so many stories of,
The secrets that they shared,
My sister kept me posted how,
Her ailing dear friend fared.

I felt as if I knew her well,
That's why I'm so upset,
I have an aching feeling for,
The Friend I Never Met.

My sister shared many stories with me about her dear friend and colleague, D Glascoe. My sister was crying when she called to tell me about D's passing. I knew I had to say goodbye in my own way.

MY FRIEND

My dearest friend has gone his way,
He's left us all behind,
And each of us will miss his soul,
So giving, pure, and kind.

Always there with helping hand,
And twinkle in his eye,
He loved to sit and reminisce,
And dream of days gone by.

His memories were joy and laughs,
Because his acts were true,
A man of honor all his life,
His character showed through.

He leaves a loving family,
And a host of loving friends,
But this is not the terminus,
Not where his story ends.

My friend will now experience,
The glory he has won,
For he will spend eternity,
With God, and God's Own Son.

Dedicated to our friend, Bud Evans, Dec. 23, 1923 – Aug. 1, 2014. An old-fashioned gentleman and a man of honor.

7

SIBLING COLLABORATIONS

I am a big fan of my sister Robin's watercolors. We have combined efforts on several occasions. The first four were challenges from her to write a poem for the painting. The next one I challenged her to create painting for the poem. The last one had no challenge, but I just decided to barge in. Lone Star Taqueria in Utah is my favorite restaurant ever. These were a lot of fun for the both of us.

THE BINDLESTIFF

He ambles down the road alone,
No special place to go,
His worldly goods upon his back,
And nothing much to show.

People turn their noses up,
And look at him askance,
Worn out jacket, floppy hat,
And knee-holes in his pants.

Rich Reardon

He doesn't seem to offer much,
No wisdom to impart,
He keeps his visions to himself,
His thoughts within his heart.

But I see something different there,
A touch of dignity,
Stalwart in his way of life,
A prince of liberty.

He doesn't strive for wealth or fame,
And no heroic deeds,
He doesn't have what others want,
But everything he needs.

A paladin of dusty roads,
For him, the perfect role,
He is the master of his fate,
And captain of his soul.

TWILIGHT

Anticipation builds in her,
Amidst the evening mist,
Soon, he'll come and join her for,
A sweet and loving tryst.

For years she's been in solitude,
Just living day by day,
Her husband's up in heaven now,
The children moved away.

But now there's opportunity,
She has a second chance,
She's found a kindred spirit for,
A twilight of romance.

She's going to risk in love again,
With all its joys and pains,
His ardent gaze reminds her that,
Her beauty still remains.

Rich Reardon

Experience is everything,
For life goes by so fast,
She's eager for the future now,
Contented with her past.

EUTERPE

Life for her is difficult,
Her problems seldom cease,
But when she calls upon the muse,
She finds a sweet release.

She strums and plucks upon the strings,
And opens up a door,
Revealing perfect beauty where,
No beauty was before.

No longer in the mundane world,
She's in a place apart,
The rhythm of the cosmos is,
The beating of her heart.

Her song is of the universe,
She echoes nature's tune,
Mysterious and subtle as,
The phases of the moon.

It's been that way since time began,
For all those many years,
So primitive, so visceral,
The Music Of The Spheres.

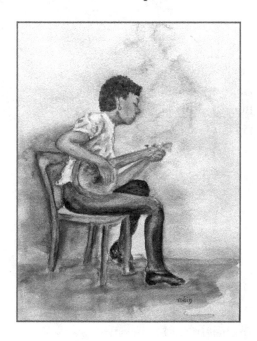

Rich Reardon

TUSCAN DREAMS

San Gimignano, Italy

Those lovely weeks in Florence,
And the rest of Tuscany,
We saw it all, at our own pace,
Just being you and me.

The glory of the Renaissance,
When beauty ruled the land,
We viewed each masterpiece in turn,
While strolling hand-in-hand.

Those days we skipped the restaurants,
With a picnic lunch instead,
With lusty wine and musty cheese,
And a loaf of crusty bread.

That town with many towers,
Each one a fortress home,
The city where the city square,
Becomes a hippodrome.

Reviewing those great times we had,
A common thread comes through.
All my dreams of Tuscany,
Are memories of you.

A GALWAY BUSKER

A cup is there in front of me,
And when the day is through,
Enough coins for my supper and,
Perhaps a pint or two.

You'll find me on the Galway streets,
An old guitar in hand,
I sing the songs of heritage,
The lost tales of the land.

Songs of mist and history,
Of heroes brave and strong,
Of all the gods who ruled us 'til,
The Right One came along.

Rich Reardon

The Fir Bolgs and Formorians,
The peoples long, long gone,
The quartet wond'rous treasures
Of Tuatha De Dannan.

The boldest name, Cu Chulain,
Who brought men to their knees,
The war skills of Achilles,
The strength of Hercules.

The noble kings of Tara,
In coats of iron mail,
Acknowledged they are righteous by,
The singing Stone of Fail.

The battle-scarred Milesians,
Or so is told the tales,
From far Iberia, o'er the seas.
In ships with cloud-white sails.

My songs are of the old times,
Of struggles lost and won,
The ancient bards my fathers,
And I'm their loyal son.

There is a universal truth,
And all fine minds concur,
Before we'll know just who we are,
We must know who we were.

LONE STAR

For a meal that is perfect,
For those on the go,
For the taste of the treasures,
Of old Mexico.

A place with great salsas,
To make your life whole,
That tingle the taste buds,
And warm up the soul.

Rich Reardon

Those perfect fish tacos,
Or beef desebrada,
Quesadillas and nachos,
Or carne asada.

Perhaps a burrito,
Or tamale's in store,
Created con brio,
And it's served con amor.

So, fill up your tummy,
With a treat that's sublime,
Just head down to Lone Star,
And squeeze on a lime.

8

PERSONAL PASSIONS

These poems reflect my love of history, literature, mythology and the Bible.

ADVENTURES

I made a trip to the gates of hell,
For my friend Enkidu,
While there, I saw Odysseus,
And Alighieri, too.

I took a nap in the Catskill range,
That lasted twenty years,
I used a lacy handkerchief,
To wipe sweet Scarlett's tears.

I watched my master tilt windmills,
With Dapple as my steed,
I laughed at Ebenezer and,
I ridiculed his greed.

Rich Reardon

I sulked and pouted in my tent,
Beside the wine dark sea,
I rafted down the Mississip,
Where Jim at last felt free.

I searched for Zion's City and,
I met the Faery Queen,
I traveled deep beneath the sea,
In Nemo's submarine.

I walked with Dr. Pangloss as he,
Spread the joyful news,
And I helped Holmes and Watson,
By discovering those clues.

I spent years at the Chateau d'If,
But my revenge was sweet,
And under Captain Disko Troop,
I joined the fishing fleet.

I fought with Robert Jordan,
In the Spanish Civil War,
I knew good Hester and her Pearl,
And what that A was for.

I rollicked in the Tabard Inn,
I heard the pilgrim's tale,
I sailed upon the Pequod and,
I chased that cursed whale.

I sought the Grail with Galahad,
So young and pure and strong,
I spent those many years alone,
'Til Friday came along.

I helped Sam Weller as he served,
The Pickwick Company,
And as the Pimpernel I worked,
To set those Frenchies free.

At Zenda I was Rassendyll,
A substitute for king,
And I saw Sam and Frodo finally,
Let go of the ring.

My life has been adventurous,
As o'er the world I'd roam,
I saw the sights, I've known the thrills,
And never left my home.

This is a poetic puzzle of sorts. I refer to many works of literature and the reader has to guess which ones they are without looking at the key. I was just thinking of the little phrases that could give the clues. How many can you identify before you check the following key?

KEY FOR ADVENTURES

Gilgamesh
The Odyssey
The Divine Comedy

Rip Van Winkle
Gone with the Wind
Don Quixote
The Christmas Carol
The Iliad
Huckleberry Finn
Pilgrim's Progress
20,000 Leagues Under the Sea
Candide
Sherlock Holmes Mysteries
The Count of Monte Cristo
Captains Courageous
For Whom the Bell Tolls
The Scarlet Letter
Canterbury Tales
Moby Dick
Le Morte D' Arthur
Robinson Crusoe
The Pickwick Papers
The Scarlet Pimpernel
The Prisoner of Zenda
The Lord of the Rings

AMERICA

What does America mean to me?
The land of the brave, the home of the free,
The gallant banner, red, white, blue,
What does America mean to you?

THE POOR POET

The Admiral of the Ocean Sea,
Finding a land where China should be,
Kitty Hawk, where man took flight,
Paul Revere, riding in the night,
The famous shot heard 'round the world,
Ft. McHenry with the flag unfurled,
The Louisiana Purchase and Fulton's Folly,
Elvis Presley and Buddy Holly,
The Mayflower Compact and Plymouth Rock,
Daniel Boone and his old flintlock,
The Constitution and the Bill of Rights,
The Golden Gate and Broadway's lights,
The soaring eagle, our national bird,
Jackie Robinson sliding into third,
Thomas Edison and Henry Ford,
Billy Graham, praising the Lord,
Guadalcanal and Bunker Hill,
Johnny Appleseed and Pecos Bill,
The Pony Express boys bringing the mail,
Herding cattle up the Chisholm Trail,
Dashiel Hammett and Ellery Queen,
Uncle Miltie and Bishop Sheen,
Andrew Jackson and John Calhoun,
Neil and Buzz out walking on the moon,
Thomas Jefferson and the Declaration,
Guiding the way to a brand new nation,
The Oregon Trail and a wagon train,
Remember the Alamo, remember the Maine,
The honored crack in the Liberty Bell,
Tecumseh Sherman saying, "War is Hell,"

Rich Reardon

"These are the times that try men's souls,"
The Great Depression and the Great Dust Bowls,
P.T. Barnum and Earth's Greatest Show,
Bob Hope's tours for the U.S.O.,
The American Odyssey – "Huckleberry Fin",
Ellis Island where they let us in,
Valley Forge and that bitter winter,
The Sultan of Swat and the Splendid Splinter,
Gold discovered at Sutter's Mill,
Belleau Wood and Pork Chop Hill,
Lewis and Clark on a three-year trip,
The Manassa Mauler and the Louisville Lip,
Lincoln at Gettysburg and his Address,
Little Round Top and the Wilderness,
Patrick Henry and Thomas Paine,
Humphrey Bogart and the Duke, John Wayne,
A shootout at the OK Corral,
"Fifteen miles on the Erie Canal,"
A picnic on the Fourth of July,
With fireworks flashing in the sky,
Doctor King, who had a dream,
The banner seen by twilight's gleam,
Captain's America and Kangaroo,
The Uncle Sam poster – "I Want You!"
General MacArthur who did return,
Liberty's torch that will always burn,
The railroads meet with a golden spike,
"Win with Wilkie," and "I like Ike,"
Manifest Destiny and elbow room,
The Unknown Soldier's hallowed tomb,

We hold our freedoms despite the cost,
Emily Dickenson and Robert Frost,
D-Day on the sixth of June,
Dancing along to a Gershwin tune,
Prairie homesteads made of sod,
A single nation under God,
The greatest country under the sun,
Remember Pearl Harbor and 9-1-1.

That's what America means to me,
The home of the brave, the land of the free,
The gallant banner, red, white, blue,
What does America mean to you?

I always wrote a poem for my company's annual convention. One year we met in Washington D.C. and I was asked to write a poem about America. After scribbling a bunch of ideas, I knew I would have to use a shotgun approach to our history. If it made it chronological, it would have a bunch of forced rhyme. My problem was how to tie it together. I woke up in the middle of the night with the first and last stanzas running through my head, so I got up and wrote most of this. I let it rest for a few days and came up with a couple more lines and that was it.

GENESIS

Brothers and sisters, gather all around,
Listen to the story, how it all began,
How the world was formed like it is today,
How the Lord created woman and a man.

Rich Reardon

First of all, there was nothing to see,
There was nothing but an endless night,
Then the Lord got tired of the murk and gloom,
So He gave the first order, "TURN ON THE LIGHT."

When the light came on there was nothing to see,
But the Lord has mysterious ways,
So He rolled up his sleeves and got real busy,
And He labored hard for six long days.

He created the seas and the land and the sun,
And the moon and the stars in the sky,
And the life with the plants and all those critters,
That walk and swim and crawl and fly.

Then He made up a man in His image out of mud,
But was sad to see him there all alone,
So He finished the job and created a woman,
He made her out of man's rib bone.

Then He put the couple in the Garden of Eden,
It was paradise where everything was free,
And He said, "YOU CAN HAVE EVERYTHING YOU
    SEE HERE,
BUT DON'T YOU TOUCH THAT APPLE TREE."

Then the Lord was finished with His six days' work,
So He went back to His home in Heaven,
And He looked down and saw that everything was good,
Then He rested there on day number seven.

Well, life was easy for the woman and the man,
Until the day when the snake strode along,
It seems snakes walked and talked back then,
So the woman didn't see nothing wrong.

And he spoke to the woman with a voice so sweet,
Saying, "Honey child, it seems a horrid waste,
Those apples are just going to rot on that old tree,
No harming if you have a little taste."

So the man and the woman took a big juicy bite,
This was sinning, and it didn't have a pardon,
The Lord got angry and He showed His full rage,
And He kicked the couple out of the garden.

That's what we call the Original Sin,
And with sinning there's a penalty to pay,
So the snake was cursed to crawl on his belly,
And he's doing that to this very day.

Woman has been saddled ever since that time,
With the agony, the pain of giving birth,
And man earns his living from his sweat and his strain,
By a plowing and a digging up the earth.

The moral of this story is a sober one indeed,
And it's better then if all the people knew it,
If the Lord tells you not to do a certain thing,
Brothers and sisters – Don't Do It!

This is written down to show us all the way,
There's more to this story – I'll tell you some day.

I enjoy studying the Bible, especially the history in the Old Testament. This was written as sort of a "rap" presentation. A minister friend of mine performed this in his church one Sunday.

DID YOU?

Did you ever fly around with Peter Pan,
    Did you duel around with Captain Hook?
Did you ever go sleuthing with Sherlock Holmes,
    Did you ever help him catch a crook?
Did you ever go rafting with Huck and Jim,
    Down the Big Muddy Mississip?
Did you ever go hiking with Lewis and Clark,
    On a three-year camping trip?

ME TOO!

Did you ever have dinner at the King's Round Table,
    Did you joust with the Mean Green Knight?
Did you ever hunt bears with Davy Crockett,
    Did you challenge Mike Fink to a fight?
Did you ever play chess with the Queen of Hearts,
    And have tea with the Hatter and the Hare?
Did you travel off to space in a great star ship,
    Just to see what was really out there?

ME TOO!

THE POOR POET

Did you ever set sail on the Hispanola,
    Did you search for the Treasure Isle?
Did you ever paint a picture with Leonardo,
    Did you see the Mona Lisa smile?
Did you slay a dragon, did you save a damsel,
    Did you wear a silver suit of mail?
Did you ever go to sea with a peg-leg captain,
      Did you help him find the Great White Whale?

    ME TOO!

Did you ever outlaw with the Younger Brothers,
    Did you rob a train with Jesse James?
And in ancient Greece, did you win a laurel wreath,
    At the original Olympic Games?
Did you talk about the galaxy with Galileo,
    Did you talk with Freud about a dream?
Did you drop that apple down on Isaac Newton,
    Did you tell James Watt about steam?

    ME TOO!

Did you get straight A's in your education,
    Were you tops at Harvard Business School?
Did you cut a great swath through the opposite sex,
    With your handsome and your dapper and your cool?
Did you make a great fortune on the Wall Street Market,
    Is a couple billion what you're worth?
Did you solve any problems, did you cure any ills,
    Did you make a better planet of this earth?

    me neither...yet

Many of us live through the adventurous books we read while our real lives are rather mundane. Actually, that's not a bad way to live.

THE BARD
A Sonnet

An evil ensign and his plot,
A butt of malmsey, a duke to drown,
A laundry basket, Falstaff caught,
Fortinbras takes up the crown.

Bianca's sister, filled with scorn,
The world's a stage and life's a play,
A brave new world for island-born,
The glory of St. Crispin's Day.

Star-crossed lovers filled with need
The Ides of March, beware, beware,
If you prick us, do we bleed?
My salad days, t'was young and fair.

A damned spot causes primal fears,
The queen's true love wears ass' ears.

A friend challenged me to write a sonnet. I decided to make the subject Shakespeare, the greatest sonneteer of them all. I took snippets and allusions from fourteen of his plays, one for each line in this sonnet. See how many you can recognize before checking the key that follows.

KEY FOR THE BARD

Othello
Richard III
The Merry Wives of Windsor
Hamlet

The Taming of the Shrew
As You Like It
The Tempest
Henry V

Romeo and Juliet
Julius Caesar
The Merchant of Venice
Antony and Cleopatra

Macbeth
A Midsummer Night's Dream

MOAB

I'm living in my memories and dreams of long ago,
Of the land that filled my childhood, and how I loved it so,
The cottonwoods in springtime, the aspens in the fall,
They held me ever thunderstruck, the beauty of it all,
Perfection unexpected in the crimson cactus rose,
That town in Spanish Valley, where the Colorado flows.

Rich Reardon

The red cliffs in their majesty, the arches made of stone,
They made me see the Purpose, and I felt it to the bone,
At night beneath the cosmos and the vast eternal plan,
Brought me closer to my Maker than cathedrals made by
    man,
To me that place was heavenly, as heaven only knows,
That town in Spanish Valley, where the Colorado flows.

I've seen so many wonders since the day that I left home,
The Grand Canals of Venice and the glory that was Rome,
I've seen the Alps at sunset and the castles on the Rhine,
But none of them can quite compare to that sweet home of
    mine,
The tempo of the canyons where the pace of living slows,
That town in Spanish Valley, where the Colorado flows.

Oh, I've been gone for many years, but do not feel apart,
That place is still inside me for there's blow sand in my heart,
And in my mind I see it still, and all the folks I knew,
It was the land and people there that taught me what is true,
They gave me needed stamina to face life's highs and lows,
That town in Spanish Valley, where the Colorado flows.

*My favorite place on the planet is my home town of Moab,
Utah. Its beauty is indescribable. I've returned many times and
was inspired to write this.*

BIBLE BABES

The Bible says they cause much strife,
Eve, Delilah, Potiphar's wife,
A man would surely live in hell,
If he were wed to Jezebel.

It seems the prophets had dim views,
That all the ladies were bad news,
A man is better off alone,
He should have kept that old rib bone.

Women tend to scheme and plot,
Try to take what man has got,
Using all their skills and wiles,
Lovely figures, lovely smiles.

But I can't live the prophet's way,
No matter what the preachers say,
Those girls are beautiful and smart,
And every day I lose my heart.

I know that biblically, I'm wrong,
I always fall for siren's song,
I don't put ladies on the shelf,
I simply cannot help myself.

Did you ever notice how women were often the problem in the
Old Testament? Ladies, this is not my idea. I'm only an observer here.

Rich Reardon

RADIO DAYS

We had no TV in my youth,
No miniature picture show,
But we had something better then,
Our Philco radio,
All of us would gather 'round,
And listen eagerly,
Each of us had favorite shows,
A close-knit family.

Henry Aldrich and Baby Snooks,
Corliss Archer and Our Miss Brooks,
The B-Bar-B boys trailing the herd,
Bergen, McCarthy, and Mortimer Snerd,
The Battling Bickersons, the Cisco Kid,
Who knew evil? The Shadow did,
Mary Noble, Backstage Wife,
Our Gal Sunday, This Is Your Life,
The Whistler was a mysterious man,
Johnny Dollar, Charlie Chan,
Arthur Godfrey's variety shows,
Captain Midnight, Major Bowes,
The Ranger, Tonto, Silver, Scout,
Fibber McGee's closet, emptied out,
Michael Shayne was always a thrill,
Judy Canova and Just Plain Bill,
Archie Andrews, a clumsy teen,
The Hornet, The Arrow, both of them Green,
Red Ryder and Thunder, showing the way,
Jack Benny, Rochester, Dennis Day,

THE POOR POET

Sky King up there, flying high,
I Was A Communist For The F.B.I.,
Amos and Andy and their Fresh Air Cab,
At Duffy's Tavern, paying the tab,
Life With Luigi, Vic and Sade,
Dragner, Nero Wolf, Sam Spade,
Jimmy Durante, Garry Moore,
Inner Sanctum's creaking door,
Stroll Allen's Alley on a sunny day,
Burns and Allen, Bob and Ray,
A Date With Judy, my love was true,
Great Gildersleeve and Fu Manchu,
Froggy the Gremlin, Bozo the Clown,
The Halls of Ivy, Young Widder Brown,
The Life of Riley, living large,
Bulldog Drummond, Myrt and Marge,
Cadet Buck Rogers, going places,
Ethel and Albert, Easy Aces,
Sweet old Beulah, the family maid,
I love a Mystery, Vic and Sade.

Oh, you can have your reality shows,
And your sitcoms and the rest,
But as for me, I'll take the past,
When radio was the best,
These days I sit and watch the tube,
An observer from my chair,
I'm not involved in any way,
But with radio – I was THERE.

This is a true geezer poem. I have such wonderful memories of those old radio shows, but my brother, a year and a half younger than me couldn't remember most of them. My sister, six years younger, didn't remember any of them. Too bad, it's their loss. Those were the glory days of theater of the imagination

THE SPIRIT

I fought with General Jackson in the swamps of New
    Orleans,
I was first to cross the Great Divide and see those magic
    scenes,
I panned for golden nuggets in the California hills,
I built the nation with the steel that I made in the mills,
I ask for no assistance but I have a helping hand,
*My names are Strength and Freedom, I'm the Spirit of the
    Land.*

In Promontory, Utah, I drove the spike of gold,
I trapped furs in the Tetons, and I shivered in the cold,
I found the lode of iron in the vast Mesabi Range,
I grew the wheat in Kansas and I helped to found the Grange,
I lost some blood and brothers on the beaches of Saipan,
*My names are Strength and Freedom, I'm the Spirit of the
    Land.*

I fished for cod and halibut way out there on the Banks,
And with McCauliffe at Bastogne I faced those German
    tanks,
From Albany to Buffalo I helped build that canal,

And in the town of Deadwood I called Bill Hickok my pal,
I played sousaphone with Sousa in his military band,
My names are Strength and Freedom, I'm the Spirit of the
  Land.

I was in the town of Philly on the day they cracked the bell,
I helped to save survivors on the day the towers fell,
I drove those dusty cattle up along the Goodnight Trail,
The Depression was a hobo as I hitched that rusty rail,
I rode with Black Jack Pershing when he crossed the Rio
  Grande,
My names are Strength and Freedom, I'm the Spirit of the
  Land.

SAUL

At Gilgal I saw victory,
As I crushed the Ammonites,
The people all proclaimed me king,
With all the royal rights.

All went well until the day,
I met that shepherd boy,
He slew the evil giant but,
He brought me little joy.

He played the harp so beautifully,
But I saw only grief,
I learned my trust had been misplaced,
I found he was a thief.

Rich Reardon

He stole the love of all the land,
That brought me happy life,
He stole the love of my best son,
My daughter for a wife.

Pride and envy were my sins,
And so, to win the day,
I tried to kill him many times,
He always got away.

I called upon the Endor hag,
To see my future gloom,
I learned upon Gilboa's heights,
That I would meet my doom.

On mountain side I faced my foe,
Abandoned by my Lord,
I lost the battle, lost my sons,
And fell upon my sword.

When citing kings of Israel,
My name is always first,
Perhaps I wasn't called the best,
But I was far from worst.

I have always thought of the biblical story of King Saul as the perfect Greek tragedy, complete with the heroic flaw.

DAVID

I saw her bathing on her roof,
Right then, my heart was lost,
I knew I had to have her soon,
No matter what the cost.

Our love was deep, our sin was great,
Her husband blocked our way,
I saw that he would lose his life,
At Rabbah that fateful day.

Our punishment was swift and strong,
The vengeance of the Lord,
The baby died, and several sons,
Were taken by the sword.

My family was dysfunctional,
And plagued by stress and strife,
One son raped his sister, and,
Another took his life.

My favorite son rebelled at me,
At the Wood of Ephriam.
He lost his life and now he dwells,
In the Kingdom yet to come.

I'm living in my dotage now,
Near the ending of my days,
I dream of all the grief and loss,
Endured for evil ways.

I think about the things I've done,
In all those days back when,
But oh that girl, that lovely girl,
I'd do it all again.

I think David, along with Joshua, were the most human characters of the Old Testament. They were both scamps. Everything went well with David until he and Bathsheba committed the great sin. His family life went badly from then on. I've often thought, however, that she was so special, he might have thought it was worth it.

THE DEVIL'S BALL

The century was finally over,
All the denizens of Hell cheered cheers,
They had a single night free of pain and fright,
And they had one every hundred years.

The Devil had a demon dance band,
At the Temple of the Evening Star,
They could play any song, play it all night long,
And of course there was an open bar.

THE POOR POET

Marquis De Sade danced the mambo,
Touting all the joys of sin,
While Al Capone sat there all alone,
And swizzled down his bath-tub gin.

Potiphar's Wife was at the mirror,
Combing out her long black hair,
Genghis Khan was busy getting it on,
With Lucrezia Borgia on a chair.

There was Jeffrey Dahmer at the snack bar,
Alfred Packer was by his side,
Attila the Hun was having his fun,
Treating Messalina as his bride.

Blackbeard the Pirate and Captain Kidd,
Were talking 'bout their years on the brine,
Emperor Nero was acting the hero,
By starting up a conga line.

Ananias told a long tall story,
Jezebel was acting the queen,
Batman's Joker was playing stud poker,
With Hitler and Idi Amin.

Bin Ladin waltzed with old Ma Barker,
Both of them were out of breath,
Richard III was flipping the bird,
At Judas and Lady Macbeth.

Pretty Boy Floyd and Billy the Kid,
Complained about their wasted youth,
Uriah Heep was acting like a creep,
Playing checkers with John Wilkes Booth.

Benedict Arnold was throwing some darts,
With Tamerlane and Simon Legree,
Muamar Khadaffi was sipping some coffee,
With Lizzie Borden on his knee.

When the grand affair was finally over,
And the flaming lights began to dim,
The Temple filled with groans and wails and moans,
For they all knew that the signs were grim.

Then the denizens returned to occupations,
Down into that deep black hole,
For another hundred years shedding sweat and tears,
And the agony of shoveling coal.

*Who would be in hell? I had fun with the internal rhyme of
the third line of each stanza.*

THE WORDS

Primeval words come down to us,
Heroic tales of yore,
Dragons slain and damsels saved,
Adventures by the score.

Gilgamesh, Sir Lancelot,
Green Knight, the Fisher King,
The fall of Troy, King Charlemagne,
The Hobbits and the ring.

These sagas are inherited,
From lands both near and far,
They burrow deep within our souls,
They're part of who we are.

Nations rise and nations fall,
Their weapons gone to rust,
Poets live and poets die,
They all return to dust.

But tales are sure and constant,
As seasons, or the tides,
The stories never go away,
The words remain, The Word abides.

Those myths, legends, and folk tales are all part of our psyche.

HARD TIMES

In the middle of the summertime of thirty-two or three,
    The Depression, it was hittin' pretty hard,
I had a little farm way out in western Oklahoma,
    I was livin' poor on cornmeal cakes and lard,
The Dust Bowl fell upon us like the wind right out of Hades,
    And the Texans got the best of all my soil,

The bankers had the mortgage rights to all the farms around
    me,
    And the Indians had rights to all the oil.

I tried real hard to make it, but I couldn't make it pay,
    On that bone-dry desolation of a land,
So on every Sunday mornin' I would holler with the
    preacher,
    For the Deity to lend us all a hand,
But the Lord, he didn't listen to our prayers and all our pleas,
    And the situation, it kept getting' worse,
'Til it seemed the only answer to our meager desperation,
    Was to hitch a final ride on some old hearse.

Now if I recall correctly, it was early in the evenin',
    'Bout the time the bitter sun was goin' down,
When I hitched the mule to my old ragged Conestoga wagon,
    And I rode the twenty dusty miles to town,
I headed for the shack behind the Santa Fe rail station,
    The place of business for old Bootleg Bill,
I plopped down fifty cents, although I scarcely could afford it,
    For a Mason fruit jar full of moonshine swill.

I guzzled as I traveled on the road back to the homestead,
    It was easy 'cause the mule, he knew the way,
There was nothin' much for me to do, just sip and hold the
    traces,
    As I felt the Conestoga bump and sway,

Now there's a funny thing about the way the juice will hit
   you,
   It's emphasized when drinkin' home-made booze,
There's times it makes you happy with the giddies and the
   grins,
   But there's times when it will kick you with the blues.

Well the blues, they hit me solid, I was feelin' pretty sorry,
   For the way that all the luck was passin' by,
The more I drank, the sorrier I saw the world around me,
   I was glad that not a soul could see me cry,
I must have gone to sleep, because the next thing I
   remember,
   I was headed for a near electric shock,
My eyes began to flutter and I saw that I was home,
   When the mule, I swear to God, began to talk.

He said, "Friend, I've heard your cryin' and your wailin' and
   your moans,
   And I think that maybe you're about to break,
So I'm about to give to you some good and wise suggestions,
   On some right and proper choices you can make,
Oh you can do the easy thing and move to Californy,
   Where the oranges are sweetenin' in the sun,
Or you can stay with me and we will whip this old
   Depression,
   And you'll have a pile of money when we're done."

Well his words, they gave me courage, and I went back to my
farm,
I worked 'til blisters formed upon my hands,
That night I made a promise that I'd make a decent livin',
On those empty, dusty, god-forsaken lands,
There's times when life will catch your dreams, and times
you just get by,
There's times when fate can only do you harm,
And that was just what happened as my roof fell in around
me,
When the bankers sold my mule and took my farm.

In days since then I've bummed around the best part of the
nation,
Been livin' with the drifters on the rails,
I've begged for all the food I eat and all the clothes I'm
wearin',
I've learned the hobo's stories and their tales,
But every night when I'm alone beneath the open heavens,
I've cursed myself for bein' such a fool,
'Cause only a dilapidated, addlepated horse's butt,
Would suck up hooch and listen to a mule.

*Sort of a tribute to the depression. I tried to get the feeling of
the times.*

A SONNET ON MY FUNERAL

My funeral happened yesterday,
I lay there for the world to see,
They had such lovely things to say,
I didn't think they spoke of me.

Many speakers took their turn,
Using wisdom, using wit,
Virtues that I did not earn,
Eschewing faults I did commit.

At times I thought the words were quaint,
Kindness reigned my whole life long,
Depicting me to be a saint,
Even though they all were wrong.

When they ignored my every sin,
I hope St. Peter listened in.

This one was inspired by the Garrison Keillor quote, "They say such nice things about people at their funerals that it makes me sad that I'm going to miss mine by just a few days."

9

FOR FAMILY AND FRIENDS

A LADY OF GRACE

A Mother is someone who's sent to begin,
A life without sorrow, a life without sin,
She brought into being a new baby boy,
Conceived and delivered with love and with joy,
And not too long after this new baby's birth,
He got the best brother and sister on earth,
Then she and our Father, with help from above,
Created a home filled with laughter and love.
That's my Mother.

A Mommy is someone who's sent down to us,
To bandage our boo-boos without any fuss,
She dries away tears and she mends our scraped knees,
She teaches us big words, like "thank you" and "please",
We learn to stand up all alone, by ourselves,
Put whining and snivels away on the shelves,
We learn to face troubles without any fear,
For all is secure because Mommy is here.
That's my Mommy.

A Mama is someone who's send down to teach,
How tall can I stand and how far can I reach?
She reads to us stories and starts us to yearn,
A love of great books and a passion to learn,
So active PTA, scouting, and fun,
And all of those meetings, she never missed one.
"Let's all make some cookies and some fudge and popcorn,"
She makes us feel glad that to her we were born.
  That's my Mama.

A Mom is a person who's God's greatest gift,
She's sent down among us to give us a lift,
She helps us to shoulder our various loads,
She helps to smooth out all the bumps in life's roads,
She's always there with us to stand by our side,
When she is around we can always feel pride,
And when it's all over and we come to the end,
I want to give thanks for my Mom, my best friend.
  That's my Mom.

*For my mom. Women go through four stages of motherhood,
from mother to mommy to momma to mom. When she heard this
poem, she was so unassuming that she had no idea it was about her.*

MOM TWO

My second mom is heaven-sent,
A halo is her crown,
She spreads her kindness and her hope,
And never wears a frown,

Her spirit is forever strong,
It's there for all to see,
A paragon of love and joy,
She's like I'd like to be.

She is a giving soul indeed,
In any way she can,
Her greatest goal in living is,
To help her fellow man,
She seldom thinks about herself,
Instead, of you and me,
A perfect person, to my mind,
She's like I'd like to be.

Dedicated to my beloved mother-in-law, Olga Scott. Knowing and loving her has been one of the greatest privileges and joys of my life.

THE SMALLEST STAR

The smallest star in the evening sky,
All lovely, lone and free,
She gradually began to rise,
To seek her destiny.

Her strength was building as she soared,
She strove to reach her goal,
All obstacles were overcome,
She had a sturdy soul.

And when she reached her apogee,
With confidence and pride,
The smallest star became the brightest star,
For the glow came from inside.

A tribute to my niece Stacey on her graduation from West-minster College.

CHAPTER TWO

The life of retirement is a wonderful one,
There's not much to do, you just lie in the sun,
No more leaving home before dawn every day,
The challenge of learning to live on half-pay.

You'll spend much more time in the Pharmacy Store,
You'll learn what Levitra and Enzyte are for,
Time in the park with those other Grand Dads,
You'll pay more attention to laxative ads.

Life becomes simple, it's no longer complex,
A good set of bowels is much better than sex,
With aches in the joints after each time you play,
And your favorite scent is the smell of Ben-Gay.

But added together, you've had a good life,
Four beautiful children, and a beautiful wife,
You've lived it with dignity, honor and pride,
You've lived it with laughter from deep down inside.

Through all of the years you have held your head high,
With feet on the ground and your face to the sky,
To retire's a beginning, it's not really an end,
And I'm glad you're my brother, I'm proud you're my friend.

This was for my brother Mike's retirement from J.C. Penney Company in 2005. I was unable to attend the celebration so I sent this. I chose very well in selecting my brother, sister, and parents. We all like each other as well as love each other.

THE TALE OF THE TARAPIN

A bunch of the boys were whooping it up,
In the Reardon house that day,
T'was Richie's birthday and the gang,
Had all come in to play.

The gifts were most abundant there,
A tie from Dad and Mom,
Six more ties from the rest of the crowd,
Old Rich was set for the prom.

The last gift was a lovely thing,
The nicest Rich ever saw,
T'was from his fruitcake sister and,
His half-assed brother-in-law.

But when he took the wrapping off,
And opened it a crack,
He peered into the darkness and,
Two turtles eyed him back.

THE POOR POET

He gently laid his gift upon,
The table made of glass,
And two hours later, there he was,
Dead drunk upon his ass.

Now when he's drunk, Ol' Rich is bad,
He'll whimper and he'll cry,
He'll moan about his lot in life,
And he'll play with his fly.

That night was special agony,
Per all the people there,
"My life needs purpose," Richie wailed,
"God damn, it isn't fair.

"I need a goal in life while on this earth,
Just something to believe,
If god would send a vision down,
I never more would grieve."

With that he passed out on his back,
'Neath the table made of glass,
And all the people there agreed,
Old Richie had no class.

Then Richie opened up his eyes,
His face looked more than odd,
"I've seen a vision from above,
Egad . . . there is a God."

Rich Reardon

"The Lord wants me to be a rake,
To be a real home wrecker,
For I have had a vision here,
And I've seen a poon and pecker."

Well since that day, there's been a change,
Old Richie's heart turned black,
He never turns some poontang down,
Nor passes up a crack.

He thinks his life has purpose now,
Just frolic, romp, and lay,
He's analyzed free love and found,
A way to make it pay.

But the under sides of turtles there,
Was all he was that night,
And he was falsely led to feel,
His actions now are right.

Who is to blame for this lost life?
The answer chokes my craw,
It is his fruitcake sister and,
His half-assed brother-in-law.

My sister and her husband gave me a pair of anatomically-correct ceramic turtles for my birthday. This was my response.

THE GIRLS OF 66

They all grew up together then,
From childhood through their teens,
There was a bond between them then,
With all that friendship means.

Camping in the Canyonlands,
Amid the Great Outdoors,
Digging smelly biffy pits,
And cooking yummy s'mores.

They all were filled with spirit then,
For the beloved Red and White,
They urged them on to victory,
With "Fight, Red Devils, Fight!"

Big dates for the Junior Prom,
Those lovely sock-hop queens,
Then heading north of town to watch,
The racing submarines.

And then they went their separate ways,
For years they've been apart,
But they've remained a group because,
There's blow-dust in each heart.

Throughout the years they've been a team,
Their bond survived the test,
Friends are gifts we give ourselves,
But old friends are the best.

My sister has maintained connections with her dear friends from grade school in Moab, Utah. They share many memories of scouting adventures with my mom as their leader. I wrote this for the "girls" when they gathered to celebrate their 60th year.

BILOXI BLUES

She went down to Biloxi, a sweet southern belle,
She was down in the south where Katrina raised hell,
The hurricane wiped out their cars and their beds,
The wind took their homes but they all blamed the feds.

But all went quite well till she decided to sit,
She sat on a spider and the wee bastard bit,
A brown recluse spider attacked the poor lass,
The bite got infected and it threatened her ass.

The doctors decided they must operate,
Remove her cute bottom before it's too late,
While the hurricane victims were cursing George Bush,
The doctors were taking a chunk of her tush.

When the ether wore off and the cutting was through,
The bad scar she has will be noticed by few,
She healed up quite well and the pain has all passed,
Though now it is said she's completely half-assed.

This was for my brother-in-law Bill Roberson's sister, Debbie Simon. She worked for the government after hurricane Katrina and was bitten on the heinie by a brown recluse spider. It was a

dangerous situation but she fortunately came out of it okay. Bill
asked me to write a poem for her and this was the result. Naturally,
she was okay before I dared to make light of it.

RANDY THREE

What a party we are having!
With friends throughout the place,
Perhaps you think that I am shy,
And afraid to show my face.

But I prefer grand entrances,
And who knows when I'll show,
I sort of like it where I am,
And I'm still not set to go.

For now, I'd like to thank you,
For every prayer and gift,
Your blessings are a comfort,
And it gives my heart a lift.

They say my name is Randy,
The third to bear that name,
Big shoes to fill, but I think I can,
And add deeds to the fame.

I'll stride among the best of them,
And take life's joyous walk,
I'll say great things, just as soon,
As I can learn to talk.

You've been so kind, I'll see you soon,
I won't wait, have no fear,
It's nice and warm where I am now,
But it sure is dark in here.

This was for a baby shower for a friend's first great-grand-
son. It was written from the point of view of the unborn baby,
thanking everyone.

VOLUNTEER

As one is moving on in life,
And learning how to live,
The greatest joys they realize,
Are when they start to give.

Whenever one can share a gift,
A lesson's there to learn,
The great reward that they receive,
Is ten-fold in return.

It's been that way since ancient times,
A tale so often told,
Tears of joy are diamond drops,
A smile the purest gold.

So give to others all your days,
A life with no regrets,
Remember that it's through the gift,
The giving giver gets.

10

POETRY GROUP CHALLENGES

I belong to a group of poets who meet once a month in Tampa. Occasionally someone will toss out a challenge for the next meeting or for a special occasion.

THE ELUSIVE MUSE

Inspiration is the key to beauty and to art,
The glory and the mysteries that set some works apart,
One needs to have a muse to help, to give their work the
    spark,
To bring light to the world around, where everything is dark.

Thalia, Urania, Polyhymnia, Erato,
Terpsichore, Euterpe, Calliope, and Clio,
Melpomene completes the list of those who must inspire,
One of them must be the tinder to create the fire.

They cover every type of art, history and dance,
Comedy and tragedy, astronomy, romance,
Hymns and all the poetry that makes our lives sublime,
Creating works of elegance that stand the test of time.

Alas, the muses did not speak, I can't do this alone,
Some of us extract the meat while I just get the bone,
The muses have abandoned me, I must admit defeat,
I cannot hold my head up high, my shame is now complete.

I will not take a chance on life, I do not have the nerve,
Others will display their skills while I will just observe,
It seems the arts are not for me, so I've made my decision,
My muse is now Sylvania, the muse of television.

For our annual Christmas banquet, the Tampa Writer's Alliance
asked me to write a poem to start the festivities. I decided to go with
the universal problem of writer's block as the theme.

PROPER POETRY

In front of crowds, I like to show 'em,
How to write a proper poem,
I can think of nothing worse,
Than those who foist on us blank verse,
Works of art should rhyme, you see,
So no more free-style poetry,
But there's one problem with my rhyming,
Every once in a while I have a little trouble with my timing.

THE POOR POET

I enjoy all types of poetry, but there are schools of thought about which is better, traditional, blank verse, free verse, etc. I prefer to write in the traditional style because I like the challenge, but that doesn't mean it is better than any others from my point of view. Also, humor is enhanced by the rhythm and the rhyme.

NOTHING MUCH

I'm going to write a poem now,
A legend of our times,
No blank verse nor a free verse work,
For neither of them rhymes.

A haiku is too short for me,
A ballad much too long,
A villanelle or clerihew,
They both seem somehow wrong.

I will not write an elegy,
Because I'm much too sunny,
I will not write a limerick,
Because I'm not that funny.

A sonnet and an ode are out,
I don't like painting scenes,
And someone please explain to me,
What terza rima means.

I guess I'm out of luck today,
I'm running out of time,
It seems I must admit defeat,
Composing a new rhyme.

At times in life you reach your goals,
At other times you miss,
I wished to build a work of art,
But ended up with this.

SUB SO-SO

All the greatest poets had deep sadness in their past,
It seems there was a catalyst that makes their verses last,
Misery's the single thread that sets their works apart,
It elevates their words up to the world of living art,
Poverty in childhood, unloved in doldrum's spell,
Their glory got its impulse from a time that's spent in Hell.

My parents didn't know this when they gave their love to me,
And thus they cursed me with the bane of mediocrity,
They stifled future brilliance with their laughter and their joy,
They gave me no good grieving which a poet can employ,
Their ignorance has doomed me with the curse of happiness,
My poems never will be good, my works are something less.

JAKE THE SNAKE

Jake the snake was swimmin' in the water,
On his way to a very hot date,
He'd found a pretty lady with the cutest little rattle,
And our hero didn't want to be late.

When he got to her lair he hollered, "Hey in there,
Do you want to come out and play?
I'm a slitherin' man with a monumental plan,
On some ways we can spend the day.

I can tell you some tales how I lost my scales,
How I broke off a part of my fang,
I can take you out for dinner on a rat or two,
Come on babe, we'll have a real bang."

Well, the lady was besotted by his silver forked tongue,
And she thought he was a sweet, sweet thing,
So she cam out to cuddle and she gave him a bite,
And boy, did that bite sure sting.

As Jake uncoiled and started to siffen,
And he saw he was losin' the light,
She said, "Some like to give a little love nibble,
But I love to give a love bite."

This challenge was to write a poem using these three words in fifteen minutes: snake, water, and sting. I see things I would change, but then it wouldn't be a fifteen-minute poem.

RAINBOWS

I'd love to bridge the gap between,
The rainbow and the child,
One's a sign of covenant,
One is gay and wild.

I know just how the rainbow works,
Through prisms and through light,
Newton taught us through his laws,
Refractions affect our sight.

A child sees rainbows differently,
With wonder and with awe,
He or she sees majesty,
They can't know Newton's Law.

They're all enthralled with Nature's world,
And rainbows give them bliss,
While I, in turn, see science there,
There's something that's amiss.

On second thought, the gap is not,
A rainbow-child affair,
The gap is here within my mind,
I don't see what is there.

Another challenge to write a poem using these three words in fifteen minutes: rainbow, bridge, and child.

GASTRIC DISTRESS
A Villanelle

I had a yummy cheese burrito,
T'was for supper yesterday,
And now I'm feeling mighty low.

The clock is ticking to and fro,
The world's no longer light and gay,
I had a yummy cheese burrito.

Feeling achy head to toe,
Tummy tumbles, bump and sway,
And now I'm feeling mighty low.

I feel like I'm about to blow,
For that short joy I now must pay,
I had a yummy cheese burrito.

Pains and gasses cause me woe,
Bursting bubbles, here I lay,
And now I'm feeling mighty low.

Excuse me please, I have to go,
I'm really sorry, cannot stay,
I had a yummy cheese burrito,
And now I'm feeling mighty low.

*As you can see, when challenged to write a villanelle, I refused
to take it seriously.*

Rich Reardon

LOWER STANDARDS

Our leader made demands on me,
A new and special rhyme,
Though sadly there were huge constraints,
He gave me little time.

But there is not a problem here,
I'll gladly save the day,
I never learned to use the time,
For thinking anyway.

So I will grab my pen and pad,
And give this chore a shot,
To try my hand at poetry,
Without a cogent thought.

I'll laugh into our leader's face,
Avoid his clever trap,
I'll show how low my standards are,
And foist on him this crap.

WASTELAND

The poet sits there at his desk,
His life is filled with pain,
Not a single thought invades,
His empty, sullen brain.

THE POOR POET

The muse is gone, the muse id dead,
There's nothing to inspire,
Flint and tinder nowhere near
No spark to light the fire..

Creative juices do not flow,
A desiccated hell,
It seems that he has blindly gone,
Too often to that well.

Oh such a horrid malady,
A pestilence, a canker,
And while the page remains a blank,
The poet's mind is blanker.

HAIKU YEAR

SPRING
> First bud of spring show,
> Nature coming back from sleep,
> Makes me sneeze - Ah-choo!

SUMMER
> School is out now,
> Summertime is upon us,
> Perspiration reigns.

Rich Reardon

AUTUMN
> Some folks call it "fall,"
> Some people call it "autumn,"
> What's the difference?

WINTER
> Snow, pristine and pure,
> Lovely, covers the landscape,
> Freezing my buns off.

11

ATTITUDE

Attitude is everything! These were written for sales meetings, but they work in real life as well. You can have a good day or a bad day—it's your choice.

HALF EMPTY OR HALF FULL

Some folks see the world as dark,
And filled with doom and gloom,
The temperature goes down a notch,
When they come in a room.

They grouse upon the smallest things,
And always seem upset,
The world owes them a happy life,
It hasn't paid up yet.

The world is out to punish them,
And life just isn't fair,
Their habit is to moan and wail,
They thrive upon despair.

These folks are very sad indeed,
They're missing life's great gift,
Miracles are everywhere,
To give the heart a lift.

Bliss is there surrounding them,
If they would stop and look,
We were meant to laugh and love,
It says so in The Book.

So my advice to all these folks,
Is try complaining less,
Misery's a habit, true,
But so is happiness.

THE JOURNEY

When nothing seems to work out right,
When you toss and turn all through the night,
When the door is locked and you can't get in,
   Grin!

When the world is out to blow your cool,
And you feel a simple low-down fool,
When end results are cut in half,
   Laugh!

When all of life seems meaningless,
When not one effort gets success,
When nothing ever seems worth while,
   Smile!

For the way to happiness in life,
Is not to wail about each strife,
And if you wear a constant frown,
It will quickly get you down,
Life is a long and bumpy road,
And all those burdens are a load,
But if you have a smile inside,
Then you can just enjoy the ride,
As every single wise man knows,
You have to stop and smell a rose,
And if you keep the journey fun,
Then when it's over, you have won.

THE DEACON

The Deacon was feeling pretty sorry for himself,
His life was on hold, put on the back shelf,
The world was all against him, life had lost its thrill,
And everything and everyone was going downhill.
Everything and everyone was going downhill.

One day it got so bad that he settled to his knees,
He started to pray, saying, "Lord, Lord, please,
Send me down a message, send me down a sign,
To help me understand this rotten life of mine.
Help me understand this rotten life of mine.

The world's become a burden, no longer worth the fight,
My days are too long and I'm frightened of the night,
My business is a failure, my family life is lame,

Please take me now Lord, I ask this in your name."
Take me now Lord, I ask this in your name.

Then the Lord looked down and He answered to the Deacon,
Saying, "Life can be a marvel if you just don't weaken,
Get up off your knees, son, stand up straight and tall,
You gotta change your attitude if you want to have it all.
You gotta change your attitude if you want to have it all.

Sure, life is full of woes and pain, you gotta understand it,
It makes you better in the end, that's the way I planned it,
It's been that way since Eden son, when facing sure defeat,
Like steel, you will be stronger when you're tempered by the
    heat.
Like steel, you will be stronger when you're tempered by the
    heat.

Miracles surround you if you'll only stop and look,
Life is to be savored son, I said so in the Book,
When Existence is a burden and you feel you've got the shaft,
Smile and grin and chuckle, let out a belly laugh.
Smile and grin and chuckle, let out a belly laugh.

The world won't give you anything that you can't handle,
So go on out and burn both ends of that old candle,
Moderation's not for you, that's for nuns and monks,
You must take big bites of life, in luscious juicy chunks.
You must take big bites of life, in luscious juicy chunks.

THE POOR POET

Face the future proudly and forget about the past,
Unfold your battle flag son, hoist it up the mast,
Attack the dangers you will face and work to come in first,
Don't worry if you come in last, not trying's even worse.
Don't worry if you come in last, not trying's even worse.

Whenever it's your time at bat, swing hard for the fences,
No matter if you swing and miss, damn the consequences,
It's better if you swing and miss than not to swing at all,
And very soon, I promise you, you'll pulverize that ball.
Very soon, I promise you, you'll pulverize that ball.

Now the Devil's gonna tempt you with all his doubts and lies,
He's gonna try to sway you and make you compromise,
But in all the years I've known him, there's one thing I have
    found,
If you look the Devil in the eye, the Devil backs down."
If you look the Devil in the eye, the Devil backs down.

Well, the Deacon rose up to his feet, a changed and better
    man,
Right then he started living in accordance with the Plan,
And when the road gets longer and the going's getting tough,
He does his best, and he has found his best is good enough.
He does his best, and he has found his best is good enough.

The moral of this story isn't very hard to spot,
To get the things you want, you gotta want the things you got,
And every word I know is true, and I will tell you why,

Rich Reardon

The Deacon told it all to me, and Deacons don't lie.
The Deacon told it all to me, and Deacons don't lie.

I performed it like a rap song at one of our gatherings. That's why the last line of each stanza is repeated.

WHO'S NEXT?

When your day is going rotten and you're feeling mighty low,
With eleven presentations done and everyone says "NO,"
When the sun is getting lower and you haven't made a sale,
When the demon imps of Doubt and Fear are biting at your
tail,
When your head is like a hammer and your tummy's full of
bile,
And you'd pay a hundred dollars just to see a person smile,
You must never let it bother you or get you all perplexed,
Merely straighten up your shoulders and shout, "WHO'S
NEXT?"

For it really doesn't matter what has happened in the past,
The next time that you demonstrate can make you wealthy
fast,
Just stay right in there trying hard and never give up hope,
'Cause the one who goes home early is a loser and a dope,
If you keep the business simple and make everyone your
friend,
It makes your days all brighter and it pays you in the end,
You will always be successful and you never will be vexed,
If you straighten up your shoulders and shout, "WHO'S
NEXT?"

THE POOR POET

Been in sales all my life and this was for an annual convention. Attitude is everything to a sales person, especially since they get so many rejections. I learned to just let it slip off my back.

THE WAY TO GO

When everything in life goes wrong,
It's time to sing a happy song,
When all your plans go up in smoke,
It's time to tell a funny joke,
When you have lost your greatest chance,
It's time to do a little dance.

Life can throw you hidden curves,
The road ahead has dips and swerves,
No matter that the deck is stacked,
What matters is how you react,
Uncertainty can chill your soul,
But attitude gives you control.

When all of life seems cold and blue,
Remember those who'd trade with you,
So stop those moans and stop those whines,
High above the sun still shines,
Just listen to that inner voice,
Good life? Bad life? It's your choice.

12

LIFE'S JOURNEYS

HOPE

Sometimes, when our stars align,
We'll have a dream come true,
Or maybe have a wish fulfilled,
And prayers are answered too.

It seems like serendipity,
When things all go our way,
It makes us feel successful,
And brightens up our day.

But vital to our daily lives,
That always helps us cope,
A prayer, a wish, a dream contains,
The miracle of hope.

It's hope that gives us fortitude,
And lets our spirits thrive,
It's hope that makes us human,
It's hope, keeps us alive.

BECOMING CIVILIZED

When I was just a tiny babe,
Like every other child,
I was a feral little imp,
All primitive and wild.

But gradually, the changes came,
My parents were the first,
To teach me that, of all my faults,
My selfishness was worst.

And then they sent me off to school,
To learn that I should care,
And when it came to other kids,
That I should always share.

They taught me to be courteous,
Obeying all the signs,
And when I colored in a book,
To stay within the lines.

A civilizing force on me,
Let others step in first,
They can have their comforts fed,
And then I'll slake my thirst.

I'm now a manufactured man,
For all the world to see,
It's been so long, I scarce recall,
That time when I was me.

PEBBLES

In the spring of life I had a plan,
I wished the world to cheer,
I wanted future folks to know,
That I had once been here.

I dreamed of great accomplishments,
Of glories in the field,
I'd outdo all my rivals and,
I simply would not yield.

Today I'm in my autumn years,
And I've achieved no fame,
No statue has my visage, nor
A plaque that bears my name.

But through the years my views have changed,
I've found a better way,
That simple kindness to someone,
Can build a better day.

The average person has his woes,
And own internal strife,
A kindness will improve his day,
And a day can change a life.

Like a pebble dropped into a pond,
And you watch the ripples flow,
So kindnesses repeat themselves,
And cause good will to grow.

I find great satisfaction now,
In recognizing worth,
And helping other folks to see,
Their value here on earth.

When winter comes, and I am gone,
I hope I've sown the seed,
I wish them to remember,
Not the doer, but the deed.

This is the philosophy of how I want to live my life. Small kindnesses can add up to something wonderful.

SMALL MEMORIES

As I grow grayer in my beard,
And I think I've seen it all,
My greatest joys are memories,
And my favorite ones are small.

The great things I've experienced,
Their importance doesn't last,
Occasionally they cross my mind,
Then fade back to the past.

But smaller memories rule my mind,
A laugh shared with a friend,
A hand held with the one I love,
Those pleasures never end.

The first car I could call my own,
A ghost tale in the dark,
A Christmas shared with family,
A picnic in the park.

When all my days are winding down,
And I'm near my final rest,
My last thoughts will be memories,
The small ones are the best.

GETTING ORGANIZED

I made a list of books to read,
I made a list of things I need,
I made a list of chores to do,
I think lists are great, don't you?

Lists are very useful things,
For who knows what the future brings,
And if intentions are declared,
Then I will always be prepared.

I can plan the days ahead,
I'll be well clad, I'll be well fed,
I'll work and play in harmony,
A master of efficiency.

But there's a problem, there's a cost,
What if all my lists are lost?
Confused and hapless I will be,
So I'll just sit and watch TV.

Karen loved making lists. Then she would make lists of her lists. She was super organized and I used to tease her that she would be lost if her lists were lost.

LIFE CYCLES

My father on his deathbed,
The family filled the room,
It was a time for sadness,
But not a time for gloom.

The functions of his body failed,
It made his bed unclean,
I helped my mother wash him,
Like the feet of Magdalene.

Now some may think it odious,
Performing such a chore,
But I did with love as he had done,
Those many years before.

He'd lived his life with dignity,
It was his given role,
The sickness took his body but,
It could not touch his soul.

We gathered at the service,
And dreamed of days gone by,
And in the back, above the choir,
I heard a baby cry.

We celebrate the loving life,
Of this good and gentle man,
He sits now at his mother's knee,
He's back where he began.

*There are three instances of cycles in this poem. My helping
my mother clean my dad like he had once done for me, the baby
crying at a funeral, and my dad sitting at his mother's knee. It seems
like all of humanity is in a cycle, what goes around comes around.*

MODERN MAN

I was raised by Gary Cooper,
I was raised by Alan Ladd,
I can never change expressions,
If I'm happy or I'm sad.

I was raised by Humphrey Bogart,
And also by John Wayne,
I can tolerate discomfort,
And never flinch with pain.

When I was in my pre-school years,
In those old days gone by,
I was told by everyone that,
Little boys don't cry.

I have a very stoic front,
I have pure nerves of steel,
I know that in the world today,
I'm not allowed to feel.

I cannot show my weaknesses,
I cannot show my fears,
I only weep when in the rain,
So no one sees my tears.

13

MAN CAVE

Ladies, enter at your own risk.

THE DISTAFF SIDE

Women are a conundrum,
Oh, they're a mystery,
They really make no sense at all,
To fellows such as me.

One moment they are happy,
The next, they've got the blues,
They have the strangest mood swings,
And what's with all those shoes?

They fret on their appearance,
And raise a lot of fuss,
They worry that their butt looks big,
When they look fine to us.

They have no sense of humor,
At least, like you and me,
They don't laugh at the Brothers Marx,
Nor at the Stooges Three.

They don't like Stan and Ollie,
They don't like Bud and Lou,
They'd rather watch a chick flick,
Does that make sense to you?

They buy the strangest objects,
For reasons no one knows,
Guest towels no one uses,
Throw pillows no one throws.

They hate a messy kitchen,
There's nothing could be worse,
They know where everything belongs,
Except down in their purse.

Yes, ladies are a strange breed,
A colossal mystery,
But they look and smell and feel good,
And that's good enough for me.

*I am fascinated by the differences between men and woman.
They are so complex and we are so simple. I sometimes think that
communications between the two sexes is still in its infancy. No
man ever understood woman and every woman understands every*

man. The trouble is, they don't believe it. They think we can't be so simple. Yes, we can.

I'M IN LOVE WITH A MEMORY

Refrain:
I'm in love with a memory,
And a memory's in love with me,
There's no place as bad as where I'm at,
Where I've been is where I want to be,
When troubled by sorrow and plagued by pain,
I just take a journey down Memory Lane,
Oh, I'm in love with a memory,
And a memory's in love with me.

Oh the girls of my youth were sweet on the tooth,
All honey and peaches and cream,
But now at this hour, the honey's turned sour,
And all I can do is to dream.

Refrain

Gone are the days when romantic plays,
Were greeted with sighs and assent,
I've recently found I'm just a bit round,
And where I was straight, now I'm bent.

Refrain

When I was a lad, all the girls thought me bad,
And not to be trusted at all,
But lately I find all the girls think me kind,
Where once it was spring, now it's fall.

Refrain

I'm old and I'm needy, decrepit and seedy,
And most of the time I'm half gassed,
But I'll find my fun and my place in the sun,
By living my life in the past.

Refrain

I know what is best, just lie down and rest,
It's no good to gripe and complain,
I'll live with life's tricks, and get all my kicks,
By traveling down Memory Lane.

A friend requested a poem with this subject. I love challenges like this.

LOVER BOY

I have a certain way with women,
They're always falling for my charms,
They are clay to me the sculptor,
Melt with passion in my arms.

Rich Reardon

Every woman is my victim,
Mine in any circumstance,
A simple nudge will urge them forward,
On to that eternal dance.

I'm oft amazed by their compliance,
They succumb so easily,
It seems they have one goal in living,
Bringing love and joy to me.

There they lay in sweet perfection,
All loveliness upon the sheet,
Breathing in anticipation,
Now I'll make their life complete.

Slowly then I build their ardor,
Starting with caress and kiss,
Toward the acme of their lifetime,
Reaching for that final bliss.

But when we reach that crucial moment,
Each to drink the loving cup,
Damn! It happens every morning,
The alarm goes off and I wake up.

In my dreams, I'm great in the sack.

RADIO LADY

I heard her on the radio,
A voice which cast a spell,
So full and rich and radiant,
With gentle charm as well.

T'was modulated perfectly,
Seductive and serene,
A sound replete with promises,
To paint a verbal scene.

I do not know her countenance,
And I don't want to know,
Illusion often is the force,
That let's the spirit grow.

But deep inside my second self,
My fantasies take flight,
And I can almost hear that voice
So softly in the night.

The lovely sweet contralto sound,
Emotions deep and true,
"That was super, Tiger Tamer,
How was it for you?"

I heard this wonderful mellifluous voice of a woman on the radio. I had sort of a crush on her right then, and thought she may look like a frog, but she sounds like Helen of Troy.

Rich Reardon

THE OOSIK

On a business trip to the Great Northwest,
  I made a stop in Nome,
I sought a little gift to take,
  To my sweet bride back home,
I wanted just the perfect gift,
  Which she would think was cute,
I wanted a reminder of,
  The land of the Aleut.

I turned down jade and turned down gold,
  I turned down reindeer bone,
No ivory, no black bear skins,
  No carvings made of stone,
But then I spied the perfect gift,
  A walrus bone of pride,
I thought t'would bring a laugh or two,
  From my sweet little bride.

The bone was slender like a wand,
  And about a foot in length,
I couldn't bend the bone a bit,
  While using all my strength,
They called the thing an oosik,
  From a giant walrus male,
And on the spot I told the clerk,
  That he had made a sale.

137

THE POOR POET

I couldn't wait to get back home,
　　And show my love her prize,
I wish you could have seen the look,
　　Of wonder in her eyes,
She asked me many questions and,
　　I answered best I could,
It made my bride feels special,
　　And it made my heart feel good.

But since that day my life has been,
　　A never-ending hell,
My bride has been comparing and,
　　I don't compare too well,
I measure up quite meagerly,
　　In stiffness and in size,
And now she's very over-fond,
　　Of her walrus oosik prize.

My bride has changed her style of life,
　　She's changed her way of dress,
She watches all those nature shows,
　　You see on P.B.S.,
She doesn't treat me royally,
　　The way she used to do,
The loving life I had before,
　　It's over, done, it's through.

So my advice to you, my friend,
  If ever you're in Nome,
Don't buy a walrus oosik for,
   Your little bride back home,
If ever you want peace in life,
   And passion in your bed,
Then buy your wife an oosik from,
  A Klondike mouse instead.

An oosik is a bone in the penis of an Alaskan walrus. When I heard about it and the wonderful sound of the word itself, the Muse struck me. Why should walruses have all the luck?

PEEWEE

I was boppin' kinda groovy to the Sarasota movie,
When no sooner did I settle in my seat,
When there was little Peewee madly cuffin' on his weewee,
He was strummin' to a boogie-woogie beat.

I said, "Hold a second son, if you'll please forgive the pun,
Why the solo to the rhythm of the band?"
He said, "I've seen a million ladies all the way from here to
     Hades,
And there's none that's quite as good as this old hand.

A gal may be a cutie, she may even be a beauty,
She may smell as sweet as honey on the vine,
But these fists are always there, I can do it anywhere,
They're the acme of convenience, 'cause they're mine.

It promotes the constitution to engage in self-pollution,
It's an exercise which helps me stay in shape,
I can do it when I please without fear of French disease,
And I never heard a finger holler rape.

Now let's stop with all this racket, let me be so I can whack it,
Let me finish with my auto-ego love,"
So I bid a soft goodbye as he fiddled with his fly,
And pursued a life that fit him like a glove.

When Peewee Herman got "caught," I couldn't let it go without a comment of some sort. Anyone with the name Peewee seemed to be asking for it.

DAMAGED GOODS

What's with all those lovely ladies,
Decorating with tattoos,
And with all those body piercings,
Ornamental bolts and screws?

Barbells stuck within their tongues,
That's confusing when they talk,
And those baubles hanging off them,
Jingle jangle when they walk.

All that ink is there forever,
Permanent and never gone,
They will tire of all that artwork,
They'll be sorry later on.

Tats and metal are distracting,
All those objects baffle me,
It seems to me they draw the eye,
Away from what I want to see.

On spoiling all that youth and beauty,
That would never be my choice,
Like bumper stickers plastered on,
A new Ferrari or Rolls Royce.

This one really shows my age. I have absolutely nothing in common with any of these people. I get tired of looking at the same picture all the time, but on my own body it would drive me crazy. Also, those body piercings would be dangerous during a thunder storm.

SAFE SEX

We'd built our mutuality 'til everything was right,
We had a tacit knowledge that tonight would be the night,
I stopped by at a pharmacy to buy a second skin,
It's best to plan for safety first when you are planning sin.

I never thought before I'd have decisions I should make,
Oh what a great dilemma and 'twas all for passion's sake,
The druggist's shelves were overstocked with brands of every
    kind,
And as I stood there gaping, why it overwhelmed my mind.

THE POOR POET

Some were made of latex skin and some with skin of lambs,
Some were small as thimble rings, and some were big as
    hams,
Some were thin or super-thin, and some were micro-thin,
And some contained a special lube to help it on and in.

They came in many colors such as some would call obscene,
Some were ripe banana-like and some were gherkin green,
Some were pink as baby's butts and some were black as coal,
And one would make me look just like an antique barber
    pole.

Some were simple to install in case I was a klutz,
Some had little warts and knobs to drive my sweetheart nuts,
Some had little finger things extending from the tip,
And some had special traction treads in case she lost her
    grip.

I couldn't face that quandary then and all ensuing strife,
It wasn't worth the trouble then to complicate my life,
I left those safety products there upon the druggist's shelf,
And had real-contact safety sex, alone and with myself.

I noticed a variety of condoms proudly displayed in a drugstore. When I was a kid there were only one or two brands, and they were kept under the counter. Now there are dozens of brands. How can you choose?

Rich Reardon

HIM OR HER

God, according to the Bible,
Is considered "Him" or "He,"
He is masculine in nature,
Never called a "Her" or "She."

This is true throughout the scriptures,
Both the Testaments agree,
Lord's Prayer doesn't say "Our Mother,"
Therefore God must be a "He."

But modern Women's Liberation,
Want's to change collective minds,
They say God must be a woman,
They have reasons of all kinds.

They say God is full of nurture,
Treats us all with loving care,
That is feminine in nature,
I can see some logic there.

But I believe that God's no woman,
I'll explain why this is true,
He'll forgive us for our failings,
Something women never do.

This one irritated some of my feminist friends. I love to do that sometimes.

THE BALLAD OF JOKEY TROY

Young Jokey Troy was a good ol' boy,
And he came from New Orleans,
He grew up long and big and strong,
On Cajun rice and beans.

His pappy's sin was moonshine gin,
His mammy was a flooze,
And every night they'd see the light,
Through Pappy's home-made booze.

Now Jokey Troy had a single joy,
In the form of the female sex,
They loved his style, the way he'd smile,
And holler out, "Who's next?"

He made each girl feel like a pearl,
Like the queen of all around,
He'd roll his eyes, she'd roll her thighs,
And they'd dance parallel to the ground.

But then one day as he made his way,
By the banks of the old bayou,
His heart felt faint when he met a saint,
By the name of Sue DePew.

Sweet Sue DePew had eyes of blue,
And hair of sunset gold,
She made old men feel young again,
She made weak men feel bold.

Rich Reardon

Though her lovely form made men feel warm,
She was pure as the morning dew,
She'd not been felt below the belt,
And her chastity was true.

When Jokey tried giving Sue a ride,
He could not reach first base,
But dead or alive, he was stuck with a drive,
That's as old as the human race.

There was just one way he could win the day,
And corrupt that sweet young thing,
He would have to cease any quest for fleece,
So he bought that girl a ring.

These days he works like those other jerks,
And he don't drink with the boys,
He returns to Sue with her eyes of blue,
And their seven little Troys.

Today his sin is moonshine gin,
And Sue's become a flooze,
But every night they see the light,
Through Jokey's home-made booze.

The first stanza popped into my head one day. It wouldn't go away so I wrote it down. It is just another of my "guy" poems.

JEZEBELLE

Miss Jezebelle Bean was a Riverboat Queen,
On the muddy waters near St. Lou,
For twenty-seven years she served stale beers,
And she fornicated with the crew.

Her orange-red hair caused everyone to stare,
It was frizzled with a two inch part,
When you saw her in the nude she was well tattooed,
With an anchor and a dragon and a heart.

She had little green eyes that concealed all lies,
With a prominent and bulbous nose,
Those years and gins gave her thirteen chins,
And you seldom saw her big mouth close.

Any thoughts of sin made Jezebelle grin,
'Cause she loved rompin' round in the sack,
For convivial rape she had a measuring tape,
Which she used on the crew on her back.

Now the captain had a charger just a little bit larger,
Than the first mate's modest spout,
But the bosun's pride was so long and wide,
That it looked like a pachyderm snout.

When Jezebelle died all the river folk cried,
You could hear them moan and wail,
They had lost their friend with the malleable end,
They had lost their source of tail.

Rich Reardon

Like a riverman's daughter she was buried in the water,
In her fanciest store-bought clothes,
But her ghost remains when you hear the refrains,
"Grab you harpoon, there she blows!"

I love the name and its nuance of evil, from the Bible. This one uses internal rhyme, too.

NETHERWORLD

Darkness is their cover cloak,
And when the sun goes down,
They skulk through backyard alleyways,
To the seedy part of town.

Into those porn emporiums,
Those paragons of sleaze,
To purchase porno magazines,
And rent those DVD's.

They sneak past racks of filth and smut,
And racks of dirty books,
While ever on the shame alert,
With constant furtive looks.

They tremble in the primal fear,
Of being recognized,
For if their secret caught the wind,
They all would be despised.

Oh, through those halls of sin and shame,
You'll never see me roam,
Because I have the internet,
In the comfort of my home.

While stopped at a traffic light one day, I noticed I was next to an adult book store and movie house. I wondered, with the Internet, why would anyone go there?

DOGHOUSE

The doghouse is my residence,
It's where I spend my time,
It is the place a fellow goes,
When he commits a crime.

I try to do the proper thing,
But sometimes I forget,
It seems I crossed the line the night,
She got her bottom wet.

They say Hell hath no fury,
Like a woman whose been crossed,
And I agree, 'cause since that night,
My loving life is lost.

I hope I've learned my lesson,
I hope I'll change that frown,
From this day forth that toilet seat,
Will always be left down.

But there remains a puzzle,
I know I'll never know,
Just why can't ladies take a peek,
Before they stop and go?

What man hasn't run afoul with the fair sex with this mistake?
It really seems to get the ladies up in arms.

14

HOMAGES

I wrote these to honor some of my favorite poets.

FELICIPEDE: THE LOVER CAT

Felicipede's a lover cat: he's called a Sneaky Pete,
No female cat is safe when he is walking down the street,
He's the bafflement of ethics groups and the A.S.P.C.A.,
For when you turn your back a sec – Felicipede's at play!

Felicipede, Felicipede, there's no one like Felicipede,
He's broken every moral law, he has a very special need,
His powers of romantic love would make you call a cop,
The moment that you look away – Felicipede's on top!
You may watch him every minute 'til you think you're going
    blind,
But I tell you, when you blink your eyes – he's sneaking up
    behind!

Felicipede's a spotted cat, with black and brown and white,
You would know him if you saw him for he's bawdy day and
   night,
He prowls the backyard alley-ways from early morn 'til late,
His tail is not the only thing that always sticks out straight,
In constant search for fresher game, new furrows to be
   plowed,
And, for a little pussy cat, he's very well endowed.

Felicipede, Felicipede, there's no one like Felicipede,
For he's a snake in feline shape, the master of the dirty deed,
You may see him by the garden gate, or near the traffic light,
But when a blue-point passes by – Felicipede's in tight!

He's a fuzzy Valentino, a Lothario with fur,
He'll chase and capture any cat (as long as it's a her),
He's no descriminator, every female has a chance,
To win a wager he will show a lady skunk his dance,
And when most folks have gone to bed and drifted off to
   sleep,
The minute that they close their eyes – Felicipede's in deep!

He cuts a swath from Dover's cliffs way up to Gretna Green,
And all those little villages and cities in between,
When screaming out his courting call, he's heard for miles
   and miles,
Like a constipated elephant who's suffering from piles,
Although he's irresponsible, he's responsible for lives,
At least ten thousand kittens by at least a thousand wives,
He's love by countless Tabby Cats, by Siamese and Manx,
And ever he's a gentleman, he always tells them "Thanks".

Felicipede, Felicipede, there's no one like Felicipede,
There never was a Cat with such a special way to spread his
seed,
He has a line that always works to make a cat say "yes",
But what that is, he'll never tell, so we can only guess,
Alas, those days are over now, no longer is he great,
He sits around and laps up cream and gets to bed by eight,
The word's gone through the neighborhood, and all reviews
are mixed,
For his master (what a bastard) had our manly hero fixed!

With apologies to Mr. Eliot

A tribute to one of my favorite poets, TS Elliot and his Old
Possum's Practical Book of Cats. *This one is an exact duplicate
of the style and rhythm and rhyme of "Macavity, the Mystery Cat."*

BOMBA DJIN

You may talk o' gin and bitters,
While the natives bear the litters,
Through the dry and dusty streets of old Bombay,
You may coldly plan the slaughter,
Of the bloke who serves you water,
Or a sissy drink, like crème de menthe frappe,
Now in Inja's sunny weather,
It was fun to get together,
To hoist a few and contemplate our sin,
And the tales of elbow benders,
Often dwell on great bartenders,
But the greatest of them all was Bomba Djin.

You had never long to linger,
As he mixed the perfect stinger,
He was quick to pour, and quicker yet to stir,
And it seemed to us ironic,
As we guzzled down his tonic,
That he's the one that always called us "Sir",
That grizzled native blighter,
With an ever-ready lighter,
To give a flame to anyone's cigar,
He was slovenly and lowly,
But by everything that's holy,
He was lord and regal master of the bar.
    It was "Djin! Djin! Djin!
You limpin' lump of sawdust, Bomba Djin,
    Mix martinis dryer,
    So to get us fellows higher,
You soggy bottle tosser, Bomba Djin.

I shan't forget the morn,
As we heard the bugler's horn,
And I thought perhaps that I was doomed to die,
I crawled from 'neath the table,
And as best as I was able,
I viewed the barroom through a jaundiced eye,
But all that I could see,
Were the signs of revelry,
Of us poor ol' sods with ne'er a chance to win,
And a'smilin' through it all,
As he swabbed the Johnny hall,
Was the cause of all our mis'ry, Bomba Djin.

It was Djin! Djin! Djin!
You sweepin' son o' Satan, Bomba Djin,
   You treated us uncouth,
   When you used too much vermouth,
You served us wet martinis, Bomba Djin.

Right then! We strung him up,
'Fore we had our mornin' sup,
And we left his carcass rottin' in the sun,
It seemed the thing to do,
But since then, I tell you true,
Our happy hours haven't been much fun,
Us misbegotten boozers,
Are a pack of bloody losers,
A new man, name of Khayaam tends the bar,
The drinks are watered down,
By that simple-minded clown,
And it costs too much, forgettin' who we are.
   For it's Djin! Djin! Djin!
You colossal docile fossil Bomba Djin,
   Though you never did deserve us,
   You never underserved us,
You're a better man than Khayaam, Bomba Djin.

With apologies to Mr. Kipling

Kipling's poem has always been a favorite and this is a tribute to him. My favorite gin, Bombay Gin, was sort of a play on words. This has the exact rhythm and rhyme style as Gunga Din.

Rich Reardon

THE EVENING MEAL

While pondering my evening meal,
I wished for foods with great appeal,
I wanted senses all to reel,
With pleasure, pleasure at the night's repast.

Ever planning, ever dreaming,
Ever plotting, ever scheming,
Spices subtle, never screaming,
The mem'ry of the night would last and last.

I would pour a fruity wine,
From the valley of the Rhine,
Also Champagne, extra fine,
Served around a floral freshette spray.

Entrecotte au Bordellaise,
Asparagus, au Hollandaise,
Pommes de Terre au Lyonnaise,
All victuals of good and grand gourmet.

Each prepared by loving hands,
Herbs from far exotic lands,
Envy of all known gourmands,
The stuff that dreams are often built upon.

As the evening meal came closer,
Paid a visit to my grocer,
And he firmly told me, "No sir,
We are out, we're out of tarragon."

THE POOR POET

What was this, this news appalling?
The scurvy knave, he must be stalling,
All my hopes and dreams were falling,
Falling on the craven grocer's floor.

To continue would be phony,
I was through with such baloney,
Ordered pizza, pepperoni,
Delivered promptly, promptly to my chamber door.

I shall gourmet Nevermore

With apologies to Mr. Poe

Sort of a tribute to Edgar Allen Poe and The Raven. Gourmet cooking has always been one of my hobbies.

LULLABY FOR DREAMLAND

Come now, little children,
Let's turn out the light,
Lay down on your pillows,
Let's go nighty-night.

You all must be happy,
And never be cross,
Think of white bunnies,
And pink candy floss.

Rich Reardon

Ignore all those vampires,
And dragons and gnomes,
They can be found in,
The finest of homes.

Those trolls in the closet,
I think they're asleep,
And werewolves have other,
Appointments to keep.

Don't fret on those monsters,
Down under your bed,
Perhaps they'll eat Mommy,
And Daddy instead.

Those giants and zombies,
And ogres and ghouls,
They all are attending,
Appropriate schools.

So think of bright rainbows,
You must concentrate,
Forget all those bad things,
Before it's too late.

I'm closing the door now,
To stifle the screams,
So goodnight little darlings,
And have pleasant dreams.

This was based on the sort of poem Shel Silverstein would have written.

RENDEZVOUS

I received the news this morning and it hit me without
    warning,
That the man I knew as Bighorn Bill had crossed the other
    side,
Then I thought of when I knew him and the way I listened to
    him,
As he told his tales and showed the world his confidence and
    pride.

In youth I took the merchant trade for all the gold that could
    be made,
I hired on with a wagon train to meet the trapper boys,
We would have a rendezvous where they would trade their
    beaver plews,
For powder, shot, tobacco, and to make a lot of noise.

That band of men, that brotherhood, oh I recall how tall they
    stood,
To be among their company and know them was a thrill,
But the man who stood so big and tall he was the greatest of
    them all,
The grizzled fellow known to all, the top man, Bighorn Bill.

At night by firelight he'd regale us all with his romantic tale,
Of a land of beauty most of us would never get to see,

Rich Reardon

Craggy tors that quickly rise under never ending skies,
And what it meant to be a man, alone and wild and free.

Of the boiling geyser fountains 'neath the ever present
    mountains,
In the place that's fit for demons, the place called Colter's
    Hell,
And the rivers and the creeks through the vast eternal peaks,
And the spirits of the nature there that held him in their
    spell.

Well, that was many years ago and as in time the ebb and
    flow,
Of life will change directions with surprises in its haste,
Demand for beaver plews went down so most of them
    moved back to town,
Except for Bill, for city living wasn't in his taste.

He built himself a cabin there among the crags and crystal
    air,
And lived life as he wanted with the mountains as his friends,
The rest of us went back to striving, ever constant in our
    driving,
In full and wild pursuit of all our goals and all our ends.

Doing what a fellow can, I've become a wealthy man,
By working, ever working, my bank accounts have grown,
I've made a pretty penny, Bighorn Bill, he hadn't any,
But Bill was quite the richest man that I have ever known.

This was a tribute to one of my favorite poets, Banjo Patterson. He is not well known in this country but he is the greatest Australian poet. He is on their ten dollar note. Most people know of some of his works, especially "Waltzing Matilda." He is the author of one of only three poems to be made into a movie: "Gunga Djin," "The Charge of the Light Brigade," and his "The Man From Snowy River." That is unless you include The Iliad, The Odyssey, or Beowulf as poems. This is an homage to one of my favorite Patterson works, "Clancy of the Overflow." I took the same rhyme and rhythm scheme and a similar theme of the joys of the wilderness as opposed to the strifes of civilization.

15

GETTING OLD

AN OLD MAN REMEMBERS

They say when one grows older that his memories grow dim,
That when it comes to full recall, the chances are quite slim,
But with such tripe I disagree, and I have much to say,
Those things that happened years ago, t'was just like
  yesterday.

I remember in my teenage years, we had that big drag-race,
Only two showed up that day, just me and What's-is-face,
I drove a bright green Chevrolet, or perhaps a yellow Ford,
It slips my mind who came in first, or how the race was
  scored.

But then we gathered up the gang to watch that football
  game,
I took along my first great love, my sweetheart What's-er-
  name,
Who'sits was our quarterback, he struggled hard and long,
I think our team came out on top, of course, I could be
  wrong.

THE POOR POET

So save your pity for someone who's not alert like me,
I'm living well within the past with my great memory,
I am not slowing down one bit, my mind is keen and clever,
My memory works perfectly, I'm as sharp as a…whatever.

BODY BEAUTIFUL

Those health nuts are a bunch of dweebs,
And doctors too, I'll bet,
They seem to think a fellow's worth,
Depends upon his sweat.

They claim that I need exercise,
That I'm no work, all play,
But they discount those efforts which,
I work at every day.

Exercising caution,
Throwing in the towel,
Jumping to conclusions,
Running off at the mouth,
Wrestling with my conscience,
Jogging my memory,
Flipping through the channels,
Going for seconds,
Pulling your leg,
Skipping the salad bar,
Pushing seventy,
Racing to the john,
Pumping irony.

I now have reached the perfect shape,
I have achieved my goal,
My body is my temple now,
My sense of worth is whole.

I will not change my regimen,
Not even if they beg,
Some folks want those six-pack abs,
I'm better, I'm a keg.

CODGER RANTS

Our culture is collapsing,
As seen on my TV,
Keep up with Kardashians?
Let them keep up with me.

I swear by all that's holy,
In heaven up above,
I'll never watch a single show,
With the words, "The Housewives of."

Life would be depressing,
And be a tragic bore,
If I should spend a single hour,
With the clods on Jersey Shore.

Instead of all that tripe, I wish,
They'd have some shows I like,
I Love Lucy, My Three Sons,
Or maybe Dick Van Dyke.

With several hundred channels,
And not a thing to watch,
I think I'll curl up with a book,
And half a case of scotch.

WHAT HAPPENED???

We're gathered here after fifty years, there's been a lot of
 laughs, been a few tears,
As we near the time out where the sidewalk ends,
All of us are moving slower, parts of us are hanging lower,
But we love the time with our oldest dearest friends.

In fifty years a lot has changed, our bodies now are
 rearranged,
And everything seems slightly out of place,
We suffer from our aches and pains, we have our stresses and
 our strains,
And we have to buy our Ben Gay by the case.

Something's happened to our hair, it's either gray or isn't
 there,
We spend our leisure cursing at our fate,
When we arise each early morn we sound like we are
 popping corn,
And when did we collect this extra weight?

In youth we had a single fashion, our lives revolved around
 our passion,
The opposite sex was a lovely thing to see,

Rich Reardon

We still can have romantic thrills, but now we need those
 little blue pills,
Our loving life depends on the pharmacy.

Aging brings out one sad fact, we're obsessed with our
 digestive tract,
And we take care of it as the best we can,
We're finding out as we grow old, working bowels are worth
 pure gold,
So we breakfast on our prunes and Raisin Bran.

Decorum now is hard to gauge, we always try to act our age,
But every now and then we just go wild,
We're all grandparents through and through, playing pull-
 my-finger and peek-a-boo,
So we never can discard that inner child.

Tonight we spend our evening here with old school spirit
 and new good cheer,
We have so many memories to share,
On the outer side we look lame, on the inside we're the same,
Those teenage kids are still down deep in there.

*This was written for my fiftieth high school reunion in 2010.
I was one of the speakers and delivered this poem. It was great to
get back together with some old friends.*

METAMORPHOSIS

We met for a cup of coffee,
My old school chum and me,
We hadn't seen each other,
For a half a century.

The man I met I didn't know,
A stranger to my eyes,
This fellow had a visage that,
I didn't recognize.

Our conversation started slow,
And stilted in its way,
We tried recalling things we did,
In years of yesterday.

But slowly, ever gradually,
I saw a change in him,
The hair returned, the wrinkles smoothed,
His body much more slim.

And there he was, the friend I knew,
It all was there to see,
By his demeanor I could tell,
He saw the same in me.

We laughed and joshed together,
With joy within each heart,
And suddenly it almost seemed,
We'd never been apart.

We finished conversations,
Started fifty years ago,
That apple-cheeked young boy I knew,
Is now the man I know.

*At my high school reunion, none of us seemed to recognize each
other at first. Gradually, the years slipped away. Maybe it was a
laugh, or the twinkle of an eye, or perhaps the way they walked,
but they became what they used to be in my eyes.*

THE OLD HOUSE

Fallen shingles, drooping roof,
Dry rot, mildew, mold,
Broken windows, broken doors,
It's sad to get this old.

Faded walls and buckled floors,
Rusty gutters sag,
Shattered fixtures, dripping sink,
Aging is a drag.

The homestead now is crumbling down,
In that, it's just like me,
If this old house could only talk,
How boring it would be.

THE EXAMINATION

I hunger for those days of yore,
Those days when I was young,
The doctors only asked one thing,
That I stick out my tongue.
But now I'm in my golden years,
I live in constant fear,
Don't want to check my tongue these days,
They want to check my rear.
I am no longer dignified,
My days of pride are through,
That used to be a private place,
But that's no longer true.
They took me in a little room,
And made me get undressed,
The temperature was twelve degrees,
So no one was impressed.
And then my fears were realized,
I knew that hope was gone,
The gloves came off the moment that,
The rubber gloves came on.
They put me on a table then,
They pulled my knees up tight,
And then they stuck their fingers in,
A place that sees no light.
They probed around for quite a while,
And took some photographs,
I think they use those pictures now,
At parties, just for laughs.

They finally let me go, and I,
Walked funny for a while,
Folks that know me say that they,
No longer see me smile.
I've never been the same since then,
My shame is now complete,
What used to be a one-way lane,
Is now a two-way street.

This is not to denigrate what the ladies go through. From day one they are invaded when they visit the doctor. For us men, however, everything goes fine until we get into our fifties and sixties, then all hell breaks loose. It is a shock to the system. By the way, women find the funniest line is about the temperature being twelve degrees. They think we men are hilarious with our insecurities.

A SONNET ON MY BALDNESS

In youth I had a mass of hair,
Every strand was in its place,
Then gradually it wasn't there,
And every day I had more face,
Such a loss is filled with grief,
Now my head reflects a shine,
As I stare in disbelief,
This gleaming skull cannot be mine,
Stranger, as you pass me by,
Please don't give a taunting jeer,
My hair has never said goodbye,
It's in my nose and in my ear,

THE POOR POET

When pondering my pristine dome,
I long for use of brush and comb.

One of the most famous sonnets of all time is John Milton's sonnet on his blindness. I thought I'd write on about my affliction . . . well, one of them anyway.

16

DINING AND DRINKING

FROMAGE

Milk is immortal when made into cheese,
The choices are hundreds and each one will please,
From cows, sheep, and goats, and buffalos too,
A gift from Olympus for me and for you.

Brick, Cheshire, Colby, Asiago and Brie,
Gorgonzola, Sap Sago make good company,
Parmesan is for royals, the experts so speak,
Without any Feta, your salad ain't Greek.

Without Mascarpone there's no tyra missou,
No Emmenthal or Gruyere? There's no Swiss fondue,
Stilton with port, there's nothing that's better,
Don't want apple pie, unless there's some Cheddar.

What good is a bagel without a Cream schmear?
Dutch Gouda and Edam are lovely with beer,
With no Camembert I would rather be dead,
Without Mozzarella, then pizza's just bread.

Cheeses have added such joys to my life,
My favorite instrument is my cheese knife,
My mouth is now happy, my tummy's content,
And Milk of Magnesia will break the cement.

"Poets have been mysteriously silent on the subject of cheese."
G.K. Chesterton

"Until now." Rich Reardon

MOLLUSKS

I had a date last evening,
Which caused my heart to sing,
I heard along the grapevine,
That she was a sure thing.

I made my preparations,
To put me in the mood,
They say that for libido,
There is a perfect food.

Oysters on the half shell,
Ensured that I would score,
I ate two dozen to be sure,
Then ate a dozen more.

My wild anticipation,
I'd start out with a kiss,
And then I'd take her to the stars,
A perfect night of bliss.

But date night was disastrous,
I felt like such a jerk,
Of all those oysters I consumed,
Not a one would work.

NECTAR OF THE GODS

Martinis are my favorite drink,
A smidgen of vermouth,
In vino there is veritas,
In gin, there's also truth.

The end results of swigging down,
This sparkling heady brew,
My jokes are all hilarious,
I also sing good too.

I feel soffisicated now,
A man about the town,
Sexier and more urbane,
The more that I drink down.

I think I'll have a couple more,
To add to my appeal,
All the girls will gather 'round,
I know just how they feel.

I feel my mind expanding through,
This drink so clean and crisp,
My wisdom now is vast, except,
Thometimes I tend to lithp.

Jutht how many have I drunk?
Wha' was the total number?
Wath it theven, wath it eight?
I rilly don' remumber.

MORNING

I plod through lumpy custard and it comes up to my knees,
The air is cold and heartless and it reeks of rotten cheese,
My hands are wearing metal gloves all smeared with
    Vaseline,
And in the night the army used my mouth for a latrine.

My eyes, they cannot focus, and my tongue, it cannot speak,
I saw my own reflection and I look a horrid freak,
Someone stuck a poster on my shoulder with a nail,
I cannot leave the bathroom now, unless I take a pail.

The world is off its axis and it wobbles to and fro,
I try my best to carry on, but it is only show,
A million evil demons sticking needles in my brain,
All joy in life is over now, for there is only pain.

Jibing laughter fills my ears, I'm now a mockery,
The whole world thinks I'm humorous, that's everyone but
    me,
I've heard it mentioned many times, today I know it's true,
Tequila shots, tequila shots, they are the Devil's brew.

Rich Reardon

ODE TO ORVILLE

A curse upon you Doubting Toms,
A pox upon you mockers,
The finest popcorn anywhere,
Is Orville Redenbacher's.

This corn will pop so big and light,
'Til o'er the lid she blows,
At parties Orville's super and,
He's great at picture shows.

So doubters better change your tune,
And mockers mend your ways,
You keep your hands off Orville's cans,
This stuff is for gourmets.

CLAN BAKE

It all started with, "Sweetheart, I've been thinking." I knew I was
in trouble when Karen started any discussion with this phrase.
She already had a plan and I had no way out. We gathered recipes
from my mother's family in honor of her mother, Anna Kolling
(Nana), who emigrated from Hungary in 1905. We bought a dozen
"blank verse" books and began filling those books by hand-writing
each of those recipes. Karen added some fun cartoons, while I
wrote poems to accompany some of the recipes. It took months.
I'll share a few excerpts.

THE POOR POET

Forward

Each of us can recall our grandmother's kitchen—the aromas and tastes which are memorable sensations of the past. Many old recipes were never written down and have been lost forever, but some have been handed down to us. This book is an attempt to preserve some of the old and to share some of the new.

This has been a labor of love and we are deeply grateful for the help which each of you gave. Hopefully, this will merely be a beginning and we can continue to share more recipes in the future.

Thank you all,
Karen and Rich
Christmas 1981

> This cook book has taken,
> An awfully long time,
> We've tried to write pretty,
> And clean up each rhyme.
>
> Our eyes have grown bleary,
> Our butts have grown flat,
> Our hands have the shakes,
> And our bellies are fat.
>
> But now that it's over,
> We'll get off our seat,
> And head for the kitchen,
> We're hungry . . . let's eat.

Rich Reardon

CHILE RELLENOS CASSEROLE

I now have reached that time of life,
That I have long been dreading,
That rubber tire around my waist,
Is scheduled for retreading.

CHICKEN DIVAN

The chicken is a feathered friend,
A truly regal fowl,
He's better than a pigeon and,
More useful than an owl.

For you can cook him many ways,
In soup or southern fried,
You really haven't lived, my friend,
Till you've been deep pot pied.

Fricasee or chicken stew,
Each one's a tasty dish,
And if you save a certain bone,
Then you can make a wish.

And where should Colonel Sanders be,
Without those noble birds,
Why he'd just be another of,
Those low Kentucky nerds.

VELVET ICING

Oh how I love to play among
Those shiny pots and pans,
And Julia Child can count me as
The biggest of her fans.

Creation in the kitchen is
The greatest of all my wishes,
But when it's over how I hate
To do those goddamn dishes.

JALAPENO CORNBREAD

I love the way these peppers go
Into my nooks and crannies,
So let's go have some cornbread and
We'll cauterize our fannies.

And if you're fond of heat and spice,
This recipe has got 'em,
It tastes so good that you won't mind
That lava in your bottom.

BEER BISCUITS

Modern life is always changing,
Everything is rearranging,
All of us have gone computer,
But I don't think we're astuter.

Rich Reardon

Micro cook and read by strobe light,
Biscuits made with Michelob light,
Rural life is turning urban,
Soon we'll sauté eggs in bourbon.

COMMUNICATION
Thrown in the "Clan Bake" just for fun.

You're made at Iran and
Those mid-Eastern meanies,
Stuff it, my sweetheart,
I'm thinking 'bout weenies.

You're steamed at the tax
On the pittance we make,
Oh, shut up, my loved one,
I'm thinking 'bout steak.

You think that Dodgers
Have too many rookies,
Go shove it, my darling,
I'm thinking 'bout cookies.

You're roasting a turkey,
It's juicy and fat,
Sit down, my beloved,
Let's have a nice chat.

17

MUSICAL NOTES

I find the evolution of music in America to be fascinating. Perhaps I'm just a frustrated lyricist.

MAMA ROOSA'S

Way down yonder in the south of Mississippi,
At the bottom of the Natchez Trace,
There's a bar and grill where they push boot swill,
And they call it Mama Roosa's Place.

The starlet of the bar is Sugar Baby Baker,
She's the sweetest little singer you could choose,
Her specialties are scat-cat and rap-slap and rhythm,
With a side bar rendition of the blues.

She has the Hunker Down Band backing up the singing,
There's Eighty-Eight Simmons on the keys,
And Rollie Kilpatrick who's a musical magician,
With his big bass fiddle 'tween his knees.

Little Sticks Maloney beats the skins like a demon,
Jimmy Jolly plays the plumbing with the slide,
And Slappy Pouquette licks the sweetest cornet,
'Cause he's getting some of Sugar on the side.

The crowds always grow when the lights go low,
Leaving Sugar Baby standing in the spot,
The Band starts lowly with soft sweet numbers,
Then they slowly move along to something hot.

As the rhythm gets quicker Mama Roosa pushes liquor,
To the characters who come to hear the sounds,
As their thirst expands to the greatest of the bands,
While the beat of Rollie's giant fiddle pounds.

When the last call is over and the crowd hits the road,
When the night starts to sounding soft and still,
Then Sugar and the boys split, taking their noise,
Leaving Mama Roosa counting up the till.

But the ghost of jazz and the spirit of the blues,
And the specter of the soul is hanging low,
The rhythm of the bass seems to echo through the Place,
'Til Mama is the final one to go.

Then the Place gets quiet through the rest of the night,
And it's silent through the best of the day,
But when the sun goes down all the people gather round,
To hear the Hunker Downs and Sugar Baby play.

Jazz and the blues are great examples of the evolution of American music styles. I finally got to use the term, "Natchez Trace," in a poem.

SECOND RATE SINGER

Watching the Grammys on the tube,
Makes me feel a bumpkin rube,
Ladies dressed like fancy dames,
Dresses made by foreign names,
Everyone has charm and class,
All those diamonds ain't no glass,
Every man there wears a tux,
And I could tell they cost big bucks.

Chorus:
    I don't want to win a Grammy,
    It's an honor, heaven knows,
    I don't want a nomination,
    'Cause I can't afford the clothes.

Oh I am a simple country boy,
Making music is my joy,
I love to strum on my guitar,
Playing songs in a cowboy bar,
A simple man with simple means,
A flannel shirt and torn blue jeans,
Worn out boots and an old slouch hat,
And I'm quite satisfied with that.

Chorus:
  I don't want to win a Grammy,
  It's an honor, heaven knows,
  I don't want a nomination,
  'Cause I can't afford the clothes.

Riding 'round in a pick-up truck,
Blaming life on my bad luck,
But everything in the truck is mine,
And so my life just suits me fine,
Small town bars in every state,
Thank the Lord I'm second-rate,
Don't bother me with fancy fluff,
I'm glad that I'm not good enough.

Chorus:
  I don't want to win a Grammy,
  It's an honor, heaven knows,
  I don't want a nomination,
  'Cause I can't afford the clothes.

BESSIE

From the foot of Lookout Mountain,
On the banks of the Tennessee,
Came a girl from deep depression,
With a spirit wild and free,
She crawled up from the gutter,
She performed in streets and bars,
From the time she was a little babe,
She was lookin' up at the stars.

Bessie, Bessie, reachin' for the golden ring,
Bessie, Oh Bessie, Lordy that girl could sing.

She learned from Old Ma Rainey,
How to polish up a song,
How to put her soul into the words,
How to bring the crowd along,
She sang of love forever gone,
Of poverty, loss, and booze,
She sang of lonely darkened roads,
She was the Empress of the Blues.

Bessie, Bessie, reachin' for the golden ring,
Bessie, Oh Bessie, Lordy that girl could sing.

And then Fate brought out a hammer,
And put out Bessie's flame,
And since that day on that highway,
The world ain't been the same,
It seems no one has filled her shoes,
No one has had the fire,
Now she has found the Promised Land,
And she's singin' up in that choir.

Bessie, Bessie, reachin' for the golden ring,
Bessie, Oh Bessie, Lordy that girl could sing.

This one came from a round-about source. I heard a hauntingly beautiful song and just had to find out who was the artist. It was Norah Jones and I became an instant fan. While browsing through

Rich Reardon

*her songs on YouTube I found a song about Bessie Smith. I loved
it and studied up on the "Empress of the Blues".*

HANK

From the cotton fields of Alabam,
To the lights of Ryman Hall,
Came along a Drifting Cowboy,
He's the greatest of them all.

Strumming on an old guitar,
He somehow learned to use,
He mixed the styles of honky tonk,
Pure country and the blues.

He climbed up all the country charts,
And soon was first in rank,
His given name was Hiram but,
The folks just called him Hank.

His songs reflected country life,
And all its aches and pains,
Of cheatin' hearts and cold cold hearts,
Of lonesomeness and trains.

Of crazy hearts and hearts with chains,
And teardrops on the rose,
Of jambalaya and crawfish pie,
And all those highs and lows.

But then one day while riding in,
A brand new Cadillac,
He was young but his heart was old,
And he never made it back.

He left behind a heritage,
To keep them on the track,
For Waylon, Willie and the boys,
And of course the Man in Black.

For all the ones who sing along,
The Grand Ole Opry way,
Though he's been gone for many years,
He still is felt today.

For showing them the way it's done,
They have one man to thank,
His given name was Hiram but,
The folks just called him Hank.

HUNGRY FOR YOU
A Country Song

CHORUS
    Darlin' I'm in love with you,
    You make everything all right,
    You are the perfect girl for me,
    You spark my appetite.

I love you more than country ham,
And more than collard greens,
More than grits and red-eye gravy,
More than rice and beans.

More than Grandma's biscuits, hon,
That's how much I love you,
I love you more than tater salad,
More than barbecue.

CHORUS

Girl, you make my taste buds sing,
The apple of my eye,
I love you more than fried catfish,
More than shoofly pie.

Sweetheart you're the ideal one,
You bring me to my knees.
I love you more than chicken fried steak,
And more than black-eyed peas.

CHORUS

You are a goddess in my mind,
You are my perfect dream,
I love you more than sweet iced tea,
And more than peach ice cream

But since I am an honest man,
And what I say is true,
I must confess that I love beer,
A little bit more than you.

CHORUS

UP YOURS, JENNY CRAIG
Sung to the tune of
"I've Grown Accustomed to Her Face"

I've grown accustomed to my fat,
I think that chubby's where it's at,
I hate a diet when I try it,
   I don't want to see my bones,
Where does lettuce get us,
   But a bod like Sherlock Holmes,
I've grown accustomed to my fat,
Accustomed to my fat, accustomed to my fat.

I've grown accustomed to my girth,
I think that girth improves my worth,
I'm all for peach parfait and cheese soufflé,
   I love those tastes and smells,
Charles Atlas may be fatless but,
   My hero's Orson Welles,
I've grown accustomed to my girth,
Accustomed to my girth, accustomed to my girth.

I've grown accustomed to my weight,
I think that fatness is my fate,
Oh how I love to sin at dinner,
    As I watch my body grow,
My belly's made of jelly,
    And my buns are oleo,
I've grown accustomed to my weight,
Accustomed to my weight, accustomed to my weight.

I've grown accustomed to my flab,
I think that skinniness is drab,
Oh who would want to feel a man of steel,
    Who wants their muscles hard,
It stinks I think to be so thin,
    I love each pound of lard,
I've grown accustomed to my flab,
Accustomed to my flab, accustomed to my flab.

TUPELO JAIL HOUSE BLUES

I got me a woman mean as can be,
She spends her time raisin' hell with me,
She gives me lip and I can't talk back,
All she's good for is givin' me flack.

I came home from work feelin' worn and beat,
Hopin' for a slab of good red meat,
I shouldn't a whopped her up side the head,
But she gave me a tofu burger instead.

THE POOR POET

I always make the wrong choice when I chose,
I got the Sittin' in the Tupelo Jail House Blues.

My woman was madder than I ever saw,
She picked up the phone and she called in the law,
The sheriff put the cuffs on and said, "Hey Sport,
You and I are headed straight down to court."

The judge on his bench looked down at me,
Sayin' "Son, you're a menace to so-ciety,
I'm givin' you five long years in jail,
Startin' right now, no chance of bail."

I've just been nailed and I got the screws,
I got the Sittin' in the Tupelo Jail House Blues.

They got no red meat in this jail,
Just bread and water and the bread is stale,
They got no wine and they got no beer,
But they don't serve tofu burgers in here.

Spend my nights behind bars and locks,
Days on the chain-gang breakin' up rocks,
Missin' the time when I was free,
And my cell-mate's taken a liking to me.

It seems like I always get bad news,
I got the Sittin' in the Tupelo Jail House Blues.

Rich Reardon

I shouldn't have given in to all that rage,
All it got me was this cold iron cage,
If ever I get out of jail alive,
My woman's waitin' there with a Colt 45.

At night I lay here behind these bars,
Talkin' to the Lord up there in the stars,
Askin' why he gave me the life I got,
And the Lord, he answered and said, "Why Not?"

I tried to win but I always lose,
I got the Sittin' in the Tupelo Jail House Blues.

18

EVANGELISTS

MALIBU, THE CHURCH OF THE HOLY PROFIT

Refrain:
Oh come to the church with the salad bar communion,
And the holy sacramental Perrier,
Singing I've got mine, now go out and get yours,
And we'll all get together some day.

There's a church in the 'burbs where the upper crust lives,
Where the sense of competition's very stiff,
Mr. Monty Ward the Third is the pastor of the flock,
But all the congregation calls him "Biff".

The pews are full of worshipers on every Sunday morn,
When the somber smell of money's pretty deep,
And everybody's looking at what everybody's wearing,
And not a soul would dare to go to sleep.

Rich Reardon

Half the people there are into real estate development,
The rest of them are pushing bonds and stocks,
When "Biff" steps up before them in a suit of silver-gray,
'Cause he doesn't look as good in priestly smocks.

He's handsome and he's slender for he works out every day,
At a spa he's been attending now for years,
He's given up cholesterol and saturated fats,
He's cut down on his alcohol and beers.

He spoke to all the people with a sermon from his soul,
He spoke of death and Hell and mortal sin,
He said, "Hell is filled with losers in the money game of life,
Friends, the only way to Heaven is to win.

You wouldn't like the management or all the print-out sheets,
You wouldn't like the bottom line of Hell,
The only clothes they let you wear must come right off the
    rack,
And they don't know how to fix cuisine nouvelle.

The gold chains we are wearing now are not allowed down
    there,
They frown upon essential signs of wealth,
No tennis courts, no foreign cars, no maids, no fancy shops,
I tell you friends that Hell is bad for health.

THE POOR POET

But Heaven, on the other hand, is quite a different tale,
The gospels tell us all the happy news,
The folks up there wear Izod shirts, have Calvin on their
    jeans,
They run around in Nike jogging shoes.

There's oat bran there for everyone, there's piles of pita bread,
All the sushi and the pasta you can eat,
You drive around in fancy cars right off the show-room floor,
And there's always lots of parking on the street.

There's tennis courts on every block, a golf course by your
    house,
And sharp boutiques just like Rodeo Drive,
There's cocktails that await you as you end a busy day,
Why it's almost like you're back with us alive.

Oh, I have had a vision where I saw the Pearly Gates,
I walked the Golden Streets with holy friends,
And I am here to tell you that the Lord, he loves the wealthy,
And that Jesus drives a new Mercedes Benz.

St. Peter plays the golf course with a seven handicap,
St. Andrew skis the clouds with all the best,
St. Matthew plays backgammon with a few of the apostles,
And Mary Magdalene regales the rest,

Rich Reardon

Now friends, I want to ask you, where would you prefer to
  live,
Tell me, what's the best location to reside,
Do you want to go below where you must walk to work each
  day,
Or would you rather go upstairs where you can ride?"

All the folks were silent, it's not dignified to shout,
And no one rolled about upon the floor,
But all the congregation thought that "Biff" had been a
  smash,
They told him so as they went out the door.

And as they left in cars that came from Germany or France,
And they headed for their separate rendezvous,
They heard the saintly voices of a pre-recorded choir,
Telling all the neighborhood the lovely news.

Refrain:
Oh come to the church with the salad bar communion,
And the holy sacramental Perrier,
Singing I've got mine, now go out and get yours,
And we'll all get together some day.

*Everyone seems to have a vision of Our Maker that fits his or
her own lifestyle. The first idea for this one came with the idea for
the salad bar communion.*

THE TENT MEETING

From out of the South came the man with the mouth,
He preached against evil and sin,
He'd rave and he'd rant, he'd foam and he'd pant,
While spittle dripped down from his chin.

His eyes were as black as a chimney sweep's sack,
His nose was a crab apple red,
He was pallid and pale, like the gut of a whale,
And his hair sprouted wild from his head.

His gaze, it was mean, and a little between,
Both a lecherous ogle and glare,
He was lanky and gaunt, just the type that would haunt,
He would make all the sinners beware.

He started out low, then his volume would grow,
'Til he filled all the tent with his might,
He snarled with his rage at this decadent age,
And consumed all the people with fright.

"Lord, heed all our prayers sent to Heaven up there,
Please slay all these sinners on earth,
Let's strike down tonight all this evil and blight,
Who've been cursed with damnation since birth."

Rich Reardon

Half the folks quivered, the rest of them shivered,
They were certain their day was at hand,
T'was abundantly clear they had reason to fear,
That their souls were all doomed on demand.

The Lord must have heard each threatening word,
For sudden clouds covered the skies,
With lightning bolts flashing and thunder booms crashing,
Then howling winds started to rise.

The storm was so loud the people all cowed,
And they fell to the floor on their knees,
The sinners all prayed while the minister brayed,
"Lord, cleanse all the world with this breeze."

When the storm finally broke, there wasn't a bloke
Who didn't think he'd been through Hell,
For the message was sent, and they knew what it meant,
With that sulphuric, brinstonish smell.

And each made a vow, that starting right now,
They'd trade all their evil for good,
And thus, they were saved, except he who'd behaved,
For the preacher was dead where he stood.

*I have always been befuddled by those hard-shell preachers
who are so unforgiving of any other beliefs. This was a poke at
their hypocrisy.*

197

THE REVEREND BILLY BOB SHEPHERD

The Reverend Mister Shepherd fluffed his hair and brushed
   his suit,
He was ready for his weekly fight with sin,
He was ready for the cameras, he would minister his flock,
He would meet the Devil and by God he'd win.

The choir was sweetly singing in their praises of the Lord,
The heart of all the audience was full,
Then the cameras saw the pulpit and great Billy Bob himself,
With his weekly, saintly, Godly brand of bull.

He gazed into the camera without flinching, without guile,
With his honest open eyes of crystal blue,
And all the congregation there and all the folks at home,
Knew that everything their shepherd said was true.

"Hear me brothers, hear me sisters, hear me sinners, hear me
   saints,
I am here to preach for Jesus to my friends,"
This was followed by "hosannahs" and a hundred "hallelujas",
And at least a hundred thousand more "amens".

"I am here to praise the Gospel, I am here to curse the
   damned,
I am here to give you sinners ghastly news,
Go to Hell you commie pinkos, all you prostitutes and gays,
All you Catholics, all you Arabs, and you Jews.

Rich Reardon

For the Bible tells us Jesus was the only son of God,
And everybody knows that Christ was white,
In the kingdom yet to come there will be room for just a few,
A few like you and me who see the light.

There's an item in the paper saying I'm a common sot,
That I have a dozen drunken driving fines,
Friends, the judge, he was a leftist and the lawyer was a Jew,
I was merely drinking sacramental wines.

And that demon imp of Satan who reported in the press,
He said I'm a lusty lecher on the make,
Folks, I never sport with animals or little girls or boys,
And I swear to God that photograph was fake.

There's a guy who claims he saw me in a gay joint down in
    town,
Playing ball games with the fellows at the bar,
He's the spawn of Ananias and he's lying through his teeth,
'Cause he knows damned well I never left my car.

And that pervert who reported I was showing off my pride,
To the little kiddies playing near the school,
I stand up here before you with my hand upon the Book
Saying he's a goddamned blasphemizing fool.

Let us bow our heads in sorrow for these sinners and their
    souls,
Let us pray for all their relatives as well,

Let us pray that they are doomed for all eternity and more,
To that endless, painful, God-forsaken Hell."

Then he dabbed his fevered forehead with a lacy scented
    cloth,
And said, "Who would like to visit God with me,
Who would like to pal around with Abraham and Moses,
I tell you friends, the journey won't be free.

We take cash, of course, and checks, of course, and money
    orders too,
We take I.O.U.'s and credit cards and stamps,
And for fifteen dollars extra we will light a holy candle,
For your mama or your uncle or your gramps."

With teary eyes he talked about the reasons for these funds,
And he urged the congregation, "Brothers GIVE,
For we have to keep our missions going all around the world,
And Heaven knows, your pastor has to live.

Just take whatever you can spare, then add a little more,
And put it in an envelope for me,
Make sure you have the postage right, then drop it in the
    mail,
Sent to Brother Shepherd, Nashville, Tennessee."

Then the minister departed and the choir began to sing,
About the ways that charity can cleanse the soul,
And Sweet Jesus up in heaven cheering all the folks to spend,
Let's help Billy Bob achieve his fiscal goal.

Rich Reardon

Then the congregation left amid that peace and all that love,
And their sense of holy purity was deep,
They looked forward to next Sunday for the time to come
    again,
When they'd watch their shepherd shear his flock of sheep.

I read a quote once that said televangelists are the pro wrestling of religion. So many of them have been "outed" as phonies that I just had to write something about it. This was especially true after the discoveries about Jim and Tammy Fae Baker and Jimmy Swaggert.

19

SPORTS

THE DUKE

Some kids cheered for Mantle, and others Willie Mays,
But as for me the Duke was king throughout my boyhood
　days,
The Dodgers were my team back then, the beloved Brooklyn
　"Bums,"
The way they faced adversity and took life as it comes.

With Hodges on the first bag and Gilliam at the key,
Peewee Reese at shortstop, and Robinson on three,
Behind the plate was Campy, the champion at home,
And way out there in right field, Furrilo used to roam.

But best of all was Snider, patrolling center field,
A fearsome Spartan warrior, with a leather glove as shield,
And when he'd swing his mighty club and put one past the
　fence,
I'd never known such thrills before, I've never known them
　since.

Well, that was many years ago, and years fly by so fast,
Some say it is a waste of time to dwell upon the past,
Ebbets Field has been torn down, its glory days are through,
There are no longer shouts of joy on Flatbush Avenue.

Yet in my mind I hear them yet on that old radio,
Remembering those happy times and screaming "Go team,
   go,"
Red Barber in his catbird seat who called the play-by-play,
But now my childhood's gone at last, the Duke died
   yesterday.

*In honor of one of my boyhood sports heroes, Edwin D. (Duke")
Snider, 1926-2001.*

THE ACE

'Twas on the thirteenth hole that day,
I had my greatest thrill,
The planets were aligned that day,
When I showed off my skill.

The sky was clear without a cloud,
An ideal day of spring,
All those lessons now paid off,
I had the perfect swing.

The ball sailed in the sky of blue,
It seemed to have a soul,
It seemed to have a purpose then,
As it headed toward that hole.

It landed on the frog hair fringe,
And then began to run,
It finally dropped into the cup,
I'd had a hole-in-one.

I'd never known such joy before,
Such bliss within my heart,
I used to be one of the mob,
But now I stood apart.

It was the best day of my life,
When skill defeated fate,
I scored the best I'd ever done,
One hundred thirty-eight.

GOLF

I had great dreams this morning,
I'd always follow through,
I'd hit long drives, I'd sink long putts,
But not one dream came true.

Tonight I am a broken man,
Like a lonely forlorn dog,
And I have come to realize,
That backwards, golf spells flog.

We had just finished a friendly scramble tournament at Towa Golf Club in Tesuque, NM, in May 2006 when a friend challenged me to write a poem about golf in less than an hour. Rich wrote this in about 20 minutes.

20

NONSENSE

MR. MCBABBAGE

Mr. McBabbage has a red cabbage,
Stuck on the end of his nose,
And Mr. McBabbage takes his red cabbage,
Whenever, wherever he goes,
The people in town and for miles all around,
Are amazed at the vegetable's size,
And all the young girls in their ribbons and curls,
Are impressed how it matches his eyes,
But Mr. McBabbage is bored with his cabbage,
Attached to the end of his snout,
"I'm sick of this crop and I'd like to swap,
For a nice little green Brussels sprout."

I heard that if you have an idea in the middle of the night, you should scribble it down right away. This was one of those. I couldn't get it out of my head, so I wrote it down so I could go back to sleep.

LIMERICKS

I prefer to let the subject matter dictate the style of the poem, but working within a template can be fun too. Here are a few.

In a whimsical moment Abe Lincoln,
To his wife said, "My dear, I've been thincoln,
With three General Grants,
We could take all of Frants,
If only he'd stop all that drincoln.

As a mathematician I'm fine,
I'm comfy with secant and sine,
But pi set at three,
Works better for me,
Than 3 point 1-4-1-5-9.

There once was an infantry colonel,
Who scribbled on day in his jolonel,
"The man said it well,
When he said war is hell,
But peace is so dull it's infolonel."

A poet of girth and diameter,
One day said, "I've found my parameter,
I'm stuck on a sonnet,
I've tried, but doggone it,
I can't write iambic pentameter."

21

LEFTOVERS

MODERN ART

I went into a gallery,
To view their grand display,
But not prepared for all the art,
I viewed with much dismay.

Thunderstruck with bafflement,
Bewildered by the scene,
A chimpanzee could do as well,
Just what could that thing mean?

Slopping, plopping, smudging, gooping,
Smirching, mucking, clouding, blobbing,
Dotting, spotting, blotching, scratching,
Clogging, dripping, dropping, globbing,

Plopping, glopping, smirching, scarring,
Tainting, blurring, soiling, clouding,
Swirling, twirling, splotching, strewing,
Dabbing, daubing, spoiling, shrouding.

But late that night I could not sleep,
There was no rest for me,
Then suddenly, I had a flash,
An art epiphany.

I saw it then, I understood,
The meaning was revealed,
Raw emotions, laid out on,
A two dimension field.

I couldn't wait to get back to,
The gallery next day,
I wanted it, regardless of,
The funds I had to pay.

A drain upon my bank account,
I gladly paid it all,
And now that work of art is there,
Ensconced upon my wall.

MUD

Election time is at our throats,
And it's becoming sad,
Accusations fill the air,
With every TV ad.

One side says the enemy,
Is saddled with a curse,
The others say the opposition's,
Plan is far, far worse.

One side has a criminal,
A pervert and a fake,
The other has a cheating man,
Who's always on the take.

It seems that only sleaze-balls run,
For offices today,
Everyone believes in crime,
And how to make it pay.

I am a frightened citizen,
I cannot sleep at night,
I have a deep suspicion now,
That both sides may be right.

There is a way to save our land,
And make our future great,
Our countrymen must stand up strong,
Before it's much too late.

When all the votes are counted and,
The final mud's been slung,
The winners should be shot at dawn,
The losers should be hung.

MY DOCTOR

I never like to see my doctor,
Even though he's very kind,
He always seems to be quite pleasant,
My health is always on his mind.

He's really very conscientious,
On my behalf, he takes great pains,
But even after all his efforts,
My hesitation still remains.

Whenever I go in his office,
Anxieties begin to rise,
And so, I've tried to understand it,
I have tried to analyze.

I think I know what makes me nervous,
Makes me feel so out of place,
It's anyone with rubber gloves on,
And one who buys them by the case.

TELEVISION COMMERCIAL

Friends, do you have gastric problems?
Tummy troubles got you down?
Strange aromas trail your movements?
Afraid to show your face in town?

Do you have to stay home often?
Feeling stuffy, feeling sick?
Doctors have the perfect answer,
Gas-No-More will do the trick.

SIDE EFFECTS MAY INCLUDE:

Rich Reardon

Acid reflux, constipation,
Baldness, blindness, diarrhea,
Shingles, rickets, beri beri,
Scurvy, jock itch, gonorrhea.

Psoriasis, and tennis elbow,,
Incontinence and fetid breath,
Rabies, acne, tonsillitis,
Post nasal drip and sometimes death.

Gas-No-More is here to serve you,
Cater to your every need,
You'll no longer feel so bloated,
Satisfaction guaranteed.

All that stress eliminated,
You'll feel you are soaring high,
Happiness will be your future
You can kiss your gas goodbye.

STRANGE ANTONYMS

I am the perfect man indeed,
Improving with my years,
Domitable, I used to be,
But now I have no fears.

These days they call me gruntled,
Corrigible and plussed,
I used to be quite maculate,
But now I'm never mussed.

I'm ruly and combobulated,
I'm sipid and make sense,
I used to be chalant at times,
But now I'm never tense.

I used to be so peccable,
But I am sheveled now,
If gainly is your goal in life,
I'll gladly show you how.

I'm petuous and consulate,
Perfection heaven-sent,
Today I am the ideal man,
At times, I'm continent.

MY GARDEN

My garden is in disarray,
There has been a recent frost,
Several plants are badly damaged,
Several plants are lost.

I see my future clearly now,
Because of that deep freeze,
Hours of daylight I'll be toiling,
Bended down on hands and knees.

Trimming, digging, grubbing, pruning,
Pulling, raking, mowing, snipping,
Crawling, smudging, hosing, mixing,
Mulching, spreading, hoeing, clipping.

Rich Reardon

Trashing, hauling, moving, shaking,
Axing, whacking, chipping, chopping,
Planting, sowing, staking, thinning,
Seed and fertilizer shopping.

On second thought, I've changed my mind,
I have found a better plan,
I will be a fan of nature,
Back to where the world began.

All that work would be a pity,
And heaven knows, I have my needs,
From this day forth my garden will be,
Filled with ornamental weeds.

A friend told me how much work she had in store for her because the winter had ravaged her garden.

FRISCO

Nestled in the bowels of the Tenderloin town,
A million miles away from Nob Hill,
There's a cavern in the wall where the denizens call,
Named the Barnacle Bar and Grill.

The establishment stands like a monumental spire,
To the nether-world of life and the scum,
Who will stoop to any sin for a pint of cheap gin,
Who will barter salvation for rum.

THE POOR POET

The Barnacle opens up at twelve o'clock noon,
But it's quiet 'til the sun goes down,
Then the action starts when a bunch of old farts,
Wander in and order up a round.

There's the Sausalito Kid, who's been called that name,
For forty-seven long, hard years,
His life as a drifter, as a shill and a grifter,
Has been dotted with a million beers.

On a stool sits Lulu, she's the sweetie of the fleet,
Thirty seasons on a hard fast track,
She made a lot of money calling sailors "Honey",
And today she wants to buy the honey back.

Over in the corner at a table set for four,
Sits a simple minded god-forsaken crowd,
What they're lacking in brains and in capital gains,
They over-compensate by being loud.

There's Chop Shop Manny and Bakersfield Bob,
And Dimple Dick from Kallamazoo,
There's Slipshod Maxie, who used to drive a taxi,
But he hasn't worked a day since sixty two.

Pouring out the nectar from behind the battered bar,
Is the evening man and mixing man Dwight,
He'll dole out the whiskey 'til you're feeling mighty frisky,
And he'll listen to your stories all night.

But when happy hour is over and the lights begin to dim,
They travel different alleys in the night,
Each meanders his ways through his own little maze,
And they cower from the coming morning light.

Then their lives go dormant through the long, long day,
As they hibernate in flop-house rooms,
Their heads go reeling as they stare at the ceiling,
And they dream about their futures and their tombs.

They remain in their comas 'til the sun goes down,
When their blood again courses their veins,
Then they gather at the Grill a million miles from the Hill,
Where the liquor and the laughter cover pains.

I had a friend who enjoyed visiting seedy bars in San Francisco.
He took me to one in particular in the afternoon, never at night.
The same people were there every time and their lives seemed to be
hopeless. I played with internal rhyme in the third line of each stanza.

GAELIC CYCLES

Bell chimes intone the hours,
Flowers grace the funeral mass,
Pass the plate and hear the pastor,
Master of the somber tones,
Moans from special mourning friends,
Ends the meeting of the throng,
Strong bodies bear the basket,

Casket slowly out the door,
Four ways to get to heaven,
Seven ways to get to hell,
Bell chimes intone the hours.....

I read about a form of ancient Irish poetry that had the last word of one line rhyme with the first word of the next line. I decided to play around with it. I kept it in Ireland and the harsh lives they led for so long.

NIGHT LIGHTS

Gleaming stars that fill the night,
Have fascinated men,
We've always wondered what they are,
And always wondered when.

Those lights began so long ago,
In spreading from their home,
Before the age of Charlemagne,
Or Caesar ruled in Rome.

Before man crawled out from the cave,
Until they reach our sight,
They crawled across the great abyss,
At the turgid speed of light.

In spying on those ancient suns,
It oft occurs to me,
That I'm not seeing things that are,
I'm watching history.